From the acclaimed author of
Things We Didn't Talk About When I Was a Girl
and *The Glass Eye,* Jeannie Vanasco's
A Silent Treatment is a searingly honest
memoir and a lasting testament to the
power of all things left unsaid.

Jeannie Vanasco's mother starts using the silent treatment not long after moving into the renovated apartment within Jeannie's home. The silences begin at any perceived slight. Her shortest period of silence lasts two weeks. Her longest, six months. As Vanasco guides us through her mother's childhood, their shared past, and the devastating silence of their present, she paints a layered, complicated portrait of a mother and daughter looking, failing, and continuing to try—in big and small ways—to understand each other. In the margins of her research, at her kitchen table with her partner, in phone calls to friends, and in delightful "hey google" queries, Vanasco explores the loneliness and isolation of silence as punishment, both in her own life and beyond it, and confronts her greatest fear: that her mother will never speak to her again.

"Articulating the pain of a removal, *something that is not there*, is massively challenging, and yet Jeannie Vanasco has done it—filled the scarcity of silence with an abundance of thrilling, exacting prose. *A Silent Treatment* is a gift for those of us who've been punished by the particular cruelty of silence and an opportunity for those who use this method of punishment to understand their frailty. A salve and a method of healing, this memoir will help countless people."

—**Marie-Helene Bertino**,
author of *Beautyland*

"Spirited in form and pensive with its subject, *A Silent Treatment* confronts both the complexity of family and the quandary of capturing a family's shape-shifting and perplexing love, their truthful and devoted love, in the amber of memoir."

—**Megha Majumdar**,
author of *A Burning*

"I look to Jeannie Vanasco to learn where memoir can go next, what psychic spaces it has yet to broach. In *A Silent Treatment*, Vanasco's response to her mom's silence unearths rage, loyalty, bottomless need, and probes the bounds of reality itself. It's impossible to read without questioning one's own primary relationships: How can we be enough to each other? How should we relate to those who love and harm us most deeply? What do we owe our parents and ourselves? Provocative, gripping, and dancing on the edge of madness, *A Silent Treatment* is a transformative thriller. I couldn't put it down, and it still hasn't let go of me."

—**Jenn Shapland**,
author of *Thin Skin*

"With each new book, Jeannie Vanasco completely reimagines what life writing can be. I am in awe of what she has done in *A Silent Treatment*, which is such a nuanced and openhearted exploration of how we tell our mothers' stories, and what it's like to be a daughter of complicated women. This is a book charged with the authority of love, a tribute without romanticization, and an indelible portrait of what can emerge from the terrifying blank space of silence."

—**Madeleine Watts**,
author of *Elegy, Southwest*

"In *A Silent Treatment*, Vanasco writes from within her mother's punitive silence, an ever-present, pressurized force that radiates through the floorboards from her apartment below. Vanasco's precise language chisels into the quiet white space of each page, conveying her urgent need to communicate while avoiding harm. In this way, the two women are mirrors to each other, caught in that age-old question: how best to love those closest to us. This is a book I'll turn to again and again, and I'm grateful Vanasco has written it."

—**Sarah Perry**,
author of *Sweet Nothings*

"Jeannie Vanasco's *A Silent Treatment* deftly explores the targeted omission of speech with both insight and compassion. In bursts of poignant, staccato prose, Vanasco lyrically traces the particular and cumulative harm of withholding. *A Silent Treatment* is a groundbreaking, complex, and moving contribution to the genre, demonstrating her unique ability to write about and through the moral complexity of our deepest intimacies."

—**Cyrus Dunham**,
author of *A Year Without a Name*

a
silent
treatment

ALSO BY JEANNIE VANASCO

*Things We Didn't Talk About
When I Was a Girl*

The Glass Eye

a silent treatment

a memoir

jeannie vanasco

TIN HOUSE
PORTLAND, OREGON

Copyright © 2025 Jeannie Vanasco

First US Edition 2025
Printed in the United States of America

All rights reserved. No part of this book may be used or reproduced
in any manner whatsoever without written permission from
the publisher except in the case of brief quotations embodied
in critical articles or reviews. For information, contact
Tin House, 2617 NW Thurman Street, Portland, OR 97210.

Manufacturing by Versa Press
Interior design by Beth Steidle

Library of Congress Cataloging-in-Publication Data is available.

Tin House
2617 NW Thurman Street, Portland, OR 97210
www.tinhouse.com

Distributed by W. W. Norton & Company

1 2 3 4 5 6 7 8 9 0

For my mom

a
silent
treatment

WRITE THE TRUTH, MY MOM TELLS ME. OTHERWISE it wouldn't be honest. Or interesting.

. . .

THE SECOND OR THIRD DAY (MAYBE)

I FORGET WORDS.

I hold a string with pieces of metal attached to it. The pieces are shaped like cats. I dangle it in front of Chris.

This is—

I pause.

I know I sound like an idiot, I continue, but the name of it. You know.

Wind chime, Chris says.

Did my mom give this to us the Easter she wasn't talking to us?

Chris can't remember, but he also can't remember if she talked to us the past two Easters.

My mom's silences—a few days here, almost six months there, over the five years since she moved in with Chris and me—amount to a year and a half, at least.

A year ago I told her: When you don't talk to me, it's all I can think about. I feel sick constantly.

Next time I do it, she said, yell at me. Tell me to go to hell.

I can't do that, I said.

Sure you can.

I'm not telling you to go to hell.

Why not?

Because. I don't know. Just don't do it again.

But she did it again. Then she did it again, again. And, now (I think), again.

I write *Start to-do list* and immediately cross it off.

Emails, checklists, those I can do.

But any writing beyond that?

About her silence? (Mom: If I didn't want you to write about it, I shouldn't have done it.)

And during her silence? (Mom: You don't need my permission.)

Enduring her silence, what I'm attempting here: to turn a painful distraction from writing into writing.

I'm not so delusional that I fail to register another impulse: to make writing its own distraction, one that prevents me from feeling my pain.

And here's something else I already did: *Start A Silent Treatment*.

But how many times have I done that?

(Mom: It's a good title.)

What if you walk down there? Chris asks.

We're sitting at the dining room table with our coffees and wind chime. He's wearing a gray shirt and boxers. The boxers are patterned with bacon and eggs, even though he's a vegetarian like me. They arrived as part of some underwear subscription service. Last month was unicorns.

Behind him, outside three narrow windows, is my mom's private stairwell. It connects her basement apartment to our shared deck. Behind me, in our dining room's far corner, is a door, probably locked. On the other side is her second set of stairs. During a silence, she climbs those only to deliver letters or holiday gifts while Chris and I sleep. (Mom: *You are such a disappointment to me. Until I can leave here, leave me alone. I want no further contact.*) One Christmas she cracked open the dining room door and tossed up my card. It flew into the room, like a magic trick, and landed on the hardwood floor.

Or we could pretend this isn't happening, I tell him. That's what I did last time, and she stopped doing it after a couple weeks.

But she can go months, he says and stands.

What are you doing?

Closing the drapes.

But she might think that means something, I say.

Why don't I try to talk to her? he says.

No, I tell him. I should do it. She's my mother.

Mother sounds cold. Its coldness feels right. She's being cold.

But *my* attached to *mother* or *mom* suddenly sounds strange. Maybe the possessiveness bothers me.

What else do I call her?

Barb sounds like what it is: a sharp projection near the tip of an arrow or hook, angled away from the main point to make extraction hard.

Barb can also be a hurtful or disparaging remark.

Barbara?

When a childhood friend addressed her mother by name, I was shocked. I still began my letters to Santa, *Dear Mr. Claus*. I expected my friend to be sent underground. (In kindergarten, I announced I was grounding myself—for what, I forget—and went to the basement.)

To you, her mother snapped, I'm Mom.

It sounded like a barb.

(Mom: A book needs conflict.)

Go to hell, I tell the wind chime. To hell with you. Why don't you go to hell?

But what would happen if I said it to her?

I'd cry. That's what I'd do.

What I'm doing.

I google *help me end the silent treatment* and am instructed not to. I am not dealing with a normal person, these online strangers claim.

But if a peer-reviewed psychology study reports that 67 percent of Americans have inflicted silence, that means 67 percent of Americans are not normal.

Well.

Duration, though. The study didn't specify duration.

Until she moved to Baltimore, we spoke on the phone almost every day. Most calls lasted an hour. She usually waited for me to call her. When she called first, she asked: Am I interrupting?

Our calls began shortly after I left Sandusky, Ohio, at eighteen, for a university near Chicago. My dad died a month later. After that, she increasingly talked about how miserable she was.

She hated her job: You know I'd make more at McDonald's than I make at the library?

She hated her house: I wish it'd burn down when the animals and I aren't home. Or I wish the city would buy it off me and turn it into a parking lot.

She missed my dad: What I wouldn't give to have him back.

She missed me: I wish I could live near you. I hate this stinking town. I'm so proud of you for getting out. I was never brave enough or smart enough.

Even our letters referenced our phone calls.

Dear Mom, Not much has happened in the four hours since I hung up with you . . .

Jeannie, Sorry about crying on the phone Sunday night . . .

(I recently found the letters—hers to me, inside a wood box underneath my office daybed, and mine to her, inside folders of official documents that she'd asked me to store—and felt relieved. They confirmed that we did get along.)

After college, I moved to New York, and for about a decade lived in a series of rent-stabilized apartments. My mom loved to visit. She'd never ridden a plane before.

I wish I could move to New York, she said. It's never boring.

She reminded me that if it ever became too expensive, I could move back home.

You wouldn't have to worry about rent or groceries, she said. You could have all day to write.

She stopped mentioning this after Chris and I started dating, but I knew the offer was still there.

After he and I moved to Baltimore for my teaching job, we rented a row house that cost the same as our New York shotgun apartment.

Now we can live in the same city, I said to her, if you still want to do that. Baltimore is so much more affordable than New York.

Then she said what she often said: I just want to be close to you.

Maybe she didn't hear me call down yesterday morning and evening. She's deaf in her left ear. Her dad blew smoke in it when she was a girl, thinking that'd cure her ear infections. If she can't see who's speaking or what's making noise, she has trouble determining where the sound is coming from, or registering a sound at all.

I turn off the air purifier (*too loud*, allege online reviews), kneel, pluck some cat hair off the area rug, and press my ear against the dining room floor.

A contractor installed insulation to muffle the noise between the first floor and the basement, which, in two months, he transformed from a dingy unfinished space into a bright apartment. My mom says the insulation works, but when Chris and I are in our dining room, we can hear if she's in her living room, watching TV, talking on the phone, or playing fetch with her dog, Max.

Is that packing tape?
    Paper crumpling?
    I should know the sound of paper crumpling. (Mom: You're the writer. You decide what to include.)

Maybe the *my* of *my mother* sounds strange because she seems strange. I doubted *my* mom would use the silent treatment again. (Mom: I won't do it again.)

Signs she's avoiding or preparing to avoid me:
- I open the door off my dining room, call down, Mom?, and she doesn't answer—even though I

heard her moving around moments ago. I shout Mom? again, and she still doesn't reply.
- She texts two-letter replies, such as *ok* and *no*.
- She locks the door off the dining room.
- She takes out her trash before sunrise.
- She sits hunched on the front steps—not the steps to our porch but the steps closest to the sidewalk (our front lawn is on a small hill)—staring off.
- She stops feeding the squirrels and birds.
- She keeps her lights off.
- She keeps her phone off.
- She stacks cardboard boxes in the laundry room or garage or on the deck. Sometimes she includes a moving checklist with the names of retirement communities hundreds of miles away in Ohio.
- She writes letters. Her cruelest claims, *We never did get along.* Her softest reads, *I love you but I think we do better at a distance.*

She never did this to me when I was a child, not that I recall.

She did it to my dad, though. They used the silent treatment on each other, she explained, because they didn't want to say something they'd regret.

What does she want to say now that she'd regret?

If I focus on one object, one without any sentimental associations, that might calm me.

The radiator, let's start there.

But is it *ray-dee-ate-er* or *rad-ee-ate-er*? I remember the realtor and the contractor pronouncing it *rad* and not *ray*. Or did they call it a *rod-ee-ate-er*? Must be regional.

As a child, I corrected my mom when she said *warsh* instead of *wash*: I warshed all your clothes and Do you need anything warshed?

I still feel horrible about that.

She also told me: I could have gone to Warshington, DC, after high school. I was a good typist. I had an offer to be a secretary, but my dad wouldn't let me. He said I'd get raped there. He said I had to get married or he was kicking me out of the house.

I sit at the dining room table and call her phone. It rings and rings below me. Frank Sinatra croons New York, New York.

I should have lied: It's impossible to make an entire song your ringtone.

When we're together and she chooses not to answer, I sometimes remind her: To make it stop, you press this button.

But when strangers glare, I want to tell them: She and my dad went dancing every Friday before I was born. When he, a longtime New Yorker, walked into the room, the DJ would play this song.

Even though he died twenty years ago, I tell my dad: I'm trying, I really am, but you know how she can be.

I remember him attempting to break her silences. Once he followed her to the basement, and I heard something smash. (Mom: He kept talking and talking. He wouldn't let it go. You wanted to transfer out of Catholic school, and I said absolutely not. So I threw the hot iron against the wall. I just wanted you to have a good education.)

I touch the doorknob the way one does in a fire and quietly test the lock. The knob turns. I open the door slightly and peer down her stairwell. The lights are off.

Mom? I want to say.

But I'm afraid to speak.

THE NEXT DAY

CHRIS AND I ARE SITTING AT THE DINING ROOM table with our morning coffees. The wind chime is still here.

I meant to put it back yesterday, I say, but I don't know when she checks the mail.

I really think we should try to end this, he says.

I turn the air purifier to its highest setting.

Psychologists say you shouldn't try to break the silence, I tell him.

I don't think that's right, he says.

They've done studies.

But not all situations, he says, are the same.

Am I being passive-aggressive if I leave her mail in the mailbox but take ours?

How about we leave the house? he asks. Go for a walk?

She might be walking Max.

So we see her, he says.

A few months ago when Chris and I had COVID, I sat here at the dining room table, and my mom stood at the top of her outside stairs, and we talked, masked, through the middle window. The first week, she texted every day:

- *How r u feeling?*
- *I put groceries at your back door.*
- *How r Chris and the cats?*
- *Do u need more soup?*

The second week, her texts dwindled to *ok* and *no*. The third week, cardboard boxes from our recycling cans appeared on the deck. Collapsed, they leaned against our wicker sofa. A rock, previously used as garden edging, kept the checklist from blowing away. *Call movers*, it said. And: *Pack*.

I told Chris: Another performance art project by my mom.

Because between *Do u need more soup?* and *Pack*, what mistake could I possibly have made?

Do you think she thinks we're lying about COVID? I asked Chris.

I'm done trying to figure it out, he said.

A few days later, we stopped testing positive, and I texted her. A couple of days after that, she stood at the middle window, asking our cats in their cat tree if they were *seeping*.

I put on an N95 mask and joined her.

How are you and Chris? she asked.

I glanced behind her, where the boxes and checklist used to be.

Better, I said.

I remembered my ultimatum after an earlier silence: If you use the silent treatment again, this living arrangement ends. I'll sell the house, and you can take the money you put into it.

Next time she does this, I thought, I'll sell the house.

But *next time* was what I thought last time.

Clean the kitchen.

Its narrow galley layout cleans quickly, and the kitchen can't be that dirty. I'm rarely in it. I never did care about cooking or baking. My mom instructed me as a child not to bother with either.

You're not ending up a housewife like me, she said.

Last night I heated a frozen pizza with the cardboard still underneath it.

I would have done the same thing, Chris lied.

(Mom: *You are such a disappointment.*)

With my earbuds in, I play my favorite podcast and start emptying the fridge. The podcast's intro music is overlaid with excerpts from author interviews. A writer says: Artists tend to put their fingers in the wounds in the silences.

Are the wounds in the silences? Or is there a meaningful pause between *wounds* and *in*? As in: Artists tend to put their fingers in wounds and in silences?

I replay the intro.

Sounds like the silences contain wounds.

Half listening to the interview that follows—*struggling with language* and *the inner workings of* and *maybe I wouldn't have written it because*—I sort food according to expired, questionable, and okay.

(Mom: *I never wanted to admit how selfish you are.*) (Mom: Don't talk to me. Don't even look at me.) (Mom: *We never did get along.*) (Mom: *I don't even know who you are anymore.*)

Nina calls.

I'm on the first floor, I whisper.

Your mom? she asks.

Yeah. I'll call you back.

Nina and I met a decade ago in New York, where she still lives. She's writing a memoir about her dad. He died last year.

I call her from my bedroom, and she says: I was actually calling about my mom. But you first.

No, you, I say. Please.

My mom was trying to guilt-trip me again, Nina says. She said, Your friend Jeannie is such a good daughter. She let her mother live with her.

Don't do it, I say.

Don't worry. I won't. I told her, It's not really working out. Jeannie and her mom aren't talking. But I didn't realize your mom wasn't talking to you again.

How'd your mom reply?

She said, Oh, okay. But she'll bring it up again. Just because a lot of Indian families do it, she thinks I'm supposed to do it too. I did finally tell her I'm writing a memoir, and she's kind of being nicer. I still get the ungrateful daughter texts, but not as many.

My mom, I say, could care less.

Oh no. Did she write you another letter?

Not yet.

What happened?

Chris's parents were in town last week, and we took them to a restaurant with stairs.

Wait, what?

His dad's knees are bad, and his mom has balance issues, but they knew about the stairs and assured us they'd be fine. They wanted barbecue. Chris and I could order two things: jackfruit and pickles. But you'd think we'd forced his parents to go.

So it's something else, Nina says.

She says she's moving.

Doesn't she say that every time?

She'd move if she could afford it. But she refuses to accept money from me. And she still insists on paying rent. I'm surprised she hasn't moved into a cardboard box underneath the interstate just so she can say, Look where my daughter put me.

I wish our moms could hang out, Nina says. They could complain about us.

They'd enjoy that, I say.

We laugh, and after we hang up, I cry.

Nina and I aren't widowed mothers.

During previous silences, my mom wrote letters claiming she planned to move:

- *I need 2 or 3 suitcases from the attic. I'm calling a moving service to move me as soon as I get an apartment. Then I'll be out of your way.*
- *I need to save some more money and have enough for movers to come and get everything and put it back together. I'll work it out.*
- *I'm trying to find an apartment and the iPad keyboard doesn't work.* (She included her iPad with this letter.)
- *I think I can get a loan to buy a mobile home. I can't find an apartment because of the pets. I'll let you know when I find something.*

Later she'd say: You've been so good to me. I was mad at myself and took it out on you. I don't really want to move.

Maybe:
- She heard *Terry* too much. Chris's dad is named Terry. My dad went by Terry.
- She found spending time with couples too hard.
- The restaurant's stairs are really the reason. Her anger can emerge when she identifies with someone she considers a victim.
- She's angry about her stairs. I've asked her many times now if her stairs bother her, and she's always replied that they're good for her.
- She's angry because we went to a barbecue restaurant. She's a vegetarian.
- I should have taken her to New Orleans.

A few days before his parents arrived, Chris and I traveled to New Orleans. I'd been invited to read from a work in progress.

But you can read something old, the event organizer said.

I'll need to do that, I said.

My mom looked after Kiffawiffick, Catullus, and Hildegard. She texted updates: *Just came down from playing with your cats Hilda I think broke the feather off the wand that was in closet they come running when I go up as soon as max takes a nap I'll go back up they cleaned their plates so I'll feed them again at noon kinda fun to be busy have fun stay safe.*

Chris and I returned to cupcakes on our dining room table. Wrapped next to them was a soap dish shaped like a cat. I opened the door off our dining room, shouted down, Mom?, and she replied, Down here. I brought gifts for her: chocolates and a glass dish shaped like the fleur-de-lis, which appears throughout New Orleans. Her favorite flower is lily of the valley.

This is beautiful, she said of the dish. I love this shade of green. It matches my love seat.

You're the one who did us a favor, I told her. You didn't have to get us anything.

It was nice to have something to do, she said.

We sat in her living room, and she asked about the trip.

That's the longest I've been away from the cats, I told her. It was weird being without them.

I know what you mean, she said. Most of the time, I want to stay here with Max.

She adopted Max—a shaggy, old, one-eyed shih tzu—last year.

She threw a cigar-shaped squeak toy, and he chased after it and carried it back. She laughed and grabbed it.

You're not allowed to smoke, she told him and threw it again.

We talked for another hour. She seemed relaxed and happy, and I felt relaxed and happy. Chris's parents arrived from Indianapolis that afternoon.

Their first day here, she told Chris's parents: When your kids are young, they give you hell. I say now it's time to give it back.

That's not exactly the most mature point of view, I said. Kids are kids after all.

I don't care if it's immature, my mom said. It's what I think.

Her tone was lighthearted. Had she not spent the past five years *giving it back*, I might have said nothing.

Okay, I said.

She seemed okay after I said, Okay.

But I should have said nothing.

But she was in a great mood the next few days.

But I still should have said nothing.

Maybe the stairs are it.

The morning after we went to the barbecue restaurant, she was unusually quiet. The five of us were at breakfast.

She insisted on paying for everyone. She pushed the receipt toward me.

You figure out the tip, she said.

That might have been the most she spoke.

Back at her apartment, she told me she needed to skip dinner. She said the food from the previous night upset her.

I'm not used to eating out, she said.

I asked if she needed medicine, and she said she needed sleep.

The next day, I overheard her on her outside stairs, complaining on the phone: Jeannie's got her windows open. Meanwhile, my fingers are freezing.

I waited ten minutes, then called down: Mom, Chris's parents are leaving soon.

Max was chomping on a squeak toy.

Mom? I'm coming down.

She was in her bedroom, feeding her cat, Brooklyn.

I can tell you're in a bad mood, I said.

I'm not, she said.

Well you seem angry, and if it's because of my open windows, I'm sorry. I didn't realize they affected you. I opened them because I'd cleaned the litter boxes.

It's not that, she said and walked away.

What is it then?

She went to her kitchen sink, and I sat on her love seat. With her back to me, she sighed.

I'm sorry I don't know, I said.

She put down her dishrag, sat in the armchair across from me, and said: It was pretty stupid to make Chris's parents climb all those stairs at dinner the other night.

That's why you're mad? They knew about the stairs.

I don't think it was right. They can't walk that well.

Their house has stairs, I reminded her. His dad's office is in their basement. He uses them every day.

I still think it was stupid.

Chris, I said, was extremely thoughtful about their visit. He researched hotels and restaurants and museums to find the most accessible. He reserved them a room next to an elevator. He drove them everywhere. He suggested other restaurants, but they wanted to go to that one. He and I don't even like barbecue.

I'm moving back to Ohio, she said. I'm unhappy here. I'm just existing. I'm calling my brother. I can go live with him in Sandusky while I look for my own place.

I almost said: The brother who banged at your door, high with a gun, and you called me at college, not knowing what to do? The brother cops warned you about? The brother you warned me about? The brother you only recently started talking to after avoiding him for thirty years?

If that's what you want, I told her. I just want you to be happy. Can you come upstairs? His parents want to say goodbye. Then we can talk about moving.

Was I supposed to beg her to stay?

The origins of her silences can seem petty:

 - Chris and I went to Home Depot without her.

- I didn't drive her to IKEA as planned because of a tornado watch.
- I called her when Chris and I were driving to dinner. I asked if she could make sure I'd blown out a candle in the dining room.
- Chris and I had COVID for three weeks.

Sometimes if I let a day pass without seeing her—a regular day, not necessarily a meaningful day (my dad's birthday, his deathday, their wedding anniversary)—she slips into a bad mood, especially if the weather is dreary like it's been this week.

I think back to that first example. I remember unloading the plants Chris and I had picked out (clematis, honeysuckle, black-eyed Susan, chrysanthemum), some of which would attract the hummingbirds she enjoyed watching. I'd also bought two birdbaths. I hid those in the garage because they were her Easter gift. I then went inside to call downstairs, but her door was locked.

She must have seen the plants on the deck—maybe when she walked Max or took out her trash—and assumed we'd ignored or forgotten her.

I texted: *We couldn't fit everything in the car in one trip. We still planned to take you today.*

I repeated this in a letter that I left in her private entryway: *I'm sorry I didn't explain our plans first. We still planned to take you to Home Depot.*

Two days later, on Easter, gift baskets sat on the dining room table. (Was that when she gave us the wind chime?) I carried her birdbaths to the yard. I placed her Easter basket next to the letter. Still tightly folded in thirds, it looked unread. Did it mean nothing to her? Was I supposed to believe it meant nothing to her? That silence lasted three months.

It's easy to say how ridiculous she was being, but it's harder, and almost unutterably heartbreaking, to see Home Depot's significance through her point of view. For Chris and me, it was another errand. She looked forward to the trip all week.

Artists tend to put their fingers in the wounds in the silences.

Or: Artists tend to put their fingers in the wounds, in the silences.

Using my phone, I visit the podcast's website. The episode's transcript doesn't include a comma after *wounds*.

But commas appear elsewhere: *There's me and then there's writer guy me, and then there's me working, which is the absence of me.*

Okay, so the wounds are in the silences.

Or: This is an and/or situation.

Artists tend to put their fingers in the wounds, in the silences, and in the wounds in the silences.

I type in my phone's Notes app: *I don't want to touch her silences. To understand her silences, I have to understand her wounds. Her silences are my wounds.*

I'm dramatic. I'm a disappointment.

Pain crowds behind my eyes and spreads to my ears.

I shouldn't have said: I can tell you're in a bad mood.

I should have said: You're right. Chris and I should have taken them to another restaurant.

I defended his judgment over hers. That might be the worst offense.

A few years ago, she said: I think I was jealous of Chris. I know that's not right of me, but I miss when it was just us.

I try the door. It's locked.

THREE DAYS LATER

I'M SITTING ALONE IN OUR CAR IN THE ALLEY behind our house. How is there this much cat hair on our dashboard? And why, in this rearview mirror, do I resemble a Catholic on Ash Wednesday?

A friend calls, asks what I'm doing.

I'm in the car, I tell her.

Oh I'll let you go.

No, no. I'm parked behind the house.

Your house?

When you're in a turn-only lane, is the turn signal necessary? Or is it redundant, like a double negative?

Are you okay?

I feel embarrassed when I'm the only one using my turn signal.

P R N 3-D 2 L

L on the gear shift stands for what exactly?

Letters: too many possibilities for too many words.

When acquaintances ask how my book is coming along, they must assume they're making small talk.

Great! I tell them because I'm sick of unsolicited writing advice:
- What you want to do is keep a spreadsheet with your word count.
- Have you heard of morning pages? There's this book called *The Artist's Way*.
- Try a writing group. Something to hold you accountable.

I slide my phone into the dash mount, open my Voice Memos app, and tap the red circle.

Whatever comes to mind, say it. I can transcribe and shape it later.

My mom's letters: too many possibilities for too many interpretations. (Mom: *I can't believe how much you have changed. I don't even know who you are anymore.*)

Wiping off the circle of dirt from my forehead, I remember what priests said on Ash Wednesday: Remember you are dust, and to dust you shall return.

I feel dead.

A therapist might say, Dead isn't a feeling.

Because the dead don't feel, do they? And isn't that what makes losing someone hard? You feel so much for someone who suddenly feels nothing at all.

But if your mother pretends that you don't exist to her and that she doesn't exist to you, how else are you supposed to describe that?

During her silences, weeds spread in our yard. I pull them on my way to somewhere else. I try to get at the root but almost never do.

But I remember, usually, to drop them before entering the car.

And I remember, usually, to wash my hands before touching my face.

I grab the weed, roll down the window.

Am I littering?

Or returning it?

I'm on a car-sized patch of stones in our alley. The weed came from the other side of our fence.

I delicately place the weed on the passenger seat.

With my right thumb, I massage my forehead.

What's wrong with me?

A friend recently told me that there was a debate online among writers. The majority, she said, bashed the present tense because, logistically, the narrator isn't narrating as they go.

I again wipe dirt off my face.

I feel committed to the present because presently I feel tense.

Some writers tell me they find it easier to write about the dead. I found it hard and horrible, no more, no less than this. Stuck in my head the weeds after: *Betrayal* rhymes with *portrayal*.
    The *weeks* after.
    Weeks after.

Weeks after my dad died, my mom and I were cleaning the garage, choosing which tools of his to donate. Sorting through mason jars of screws and nails, I found a single sheet of paper folded and rolled up. I recognized her cursive.
    I bet it's his fault his first marriage ended.
    I didn't read much of it, I said and handed it to her.
    She skimmed it, said: Throw it away.
    I remember thinking, You don't get to take it back.

I thought about the morning pages. I did.

The L on this gear shift, I should know it.

Low, Google answers.

When have I ever used low gear?

Did any engineers dispute its placement on the gear shift? Or was this design unanimous?

Obviously *low* belongs lower than the rest. (Mom: *You always treated me like I was beneath you.*)

I start the car. The MAINT REQD symbol lights up.

She told me to schedule a car inspection.

And wiper fluid, she said we needed wiper fluid.

If I can't perform minor tasks for her, why do I continue attempting a major one?

Nobody needs me, she said—after which silence, I forget.

We were at a restaurant down the street from our house, just the two of us. Our table was against a big window, and she was staring at the flat, empty surface between us.

I'm old, she said. My life is behind me. Your dad is gone. You're doing well, and I'm happy for that. But I have nothing to offer anyone. I feel like I don't have a purpose.

Would a book give you purpose? I asked. A book I'd write for you. About you.

But I'm not interesting.

You are interesting. To do it, though, I'd need your help.

Would you interview me?

Would that be okay?

Yes, she said. I'd like that.

Do you think there's any relationship between your silences and your abusive childhood? Your abusive first marriage? What's your day-to-day experience when using the silent treatment? What are you feeling right now? What can I do to prevent this from happening again?

(Mom: You didn't do anything wrong. I didn't have to behave the way I did. I take full responsibility for my actions.)

In my rearview mirror, our busybody neighbor approaches. The first week Chris and I lived here, somebody tried to break into our house. She blamed our lack of drapes.

I press my phone against my ear.

She knocks on the passenger window. I point at my phone.

What's that? I say into the phone.

She motions for me to roll down my window.

I continue: Oh that's terrible.

She knocks again.

Hold on, I tell the phone.

I roll down the window.

You have to bag things, she says, before throwing them in your trash can.

I do, I tell her.

You don't always, she says. There was a pillow in there that wasn't bagged.

I don't know where that came from. Maybe somebody walking by.

With a pillow? she says.

I really have to get back to this call. I'm very sorry. I don't mean to be rude.

What's that? she asks, looking at the weed.

A weed, I tell her and roll up the window.

I slip the phone back into the dash mount.

You're on speaker.

Should I have started, as I once did, with one of my earliest memories? In it, I'm handing my mom a small paper cup of dandelions.

They're beautiful, she says.

When did I learn they were weeds?

There was a daisy print on the paper cup holding the dandelions. I remember only because I swished water from these disposable cups every day after brushing my teeth.

Or maybe there were no daisies.

I suppose it doesn't matter.

What matters is her happiness about the dandelions.

What matters is her happiness about this book.

I need to remember: She knows about this project, its title and premise—has known its title and premise for almost two years now, and in that time how many times have I asked her for permission? (Mom: You don't need to keep asking. You're the writer. You write what you need to write.)

Months ago I published an essay about her silent treatment. I asked her many times to read the essay before it moved too far along in the editorial process.

If you read it, I said, and don't want me to publish it, I won't.

I want to be surprised, she told me.

But it's about your silent treatment, I said.

I think you should write about it, she said. And anyway, it's the truth.

After the essay reached layout, she spoke to a fact-checker.

She told me: I said to the fact-checker, Whatever my daughter wrote is the truth.

After the essay was published, she said: Seeing it in print, I realize it was kind of stupid what I did.

Some negative comments arrived. Their general critique: How dare I write about her silent treatment, and why didn't I help her get involved in the community?

I told her about these comments.

Tell them that you did try to help me, she said.

It's better not to engage, I said.

But they've got it all wrong, she said.

Secretly, I felt pleased. She felt protective of me. This allowed her to embrace the role of a mother.

Maybe:
- She's trying to help me because she believes, as I do, that her silences can help me understand her life, and her life can help me understand her silences, and this tension can answer the questions most repeated in my notebooks: *Book about my mom? Book for my mom? How do I write a book for and about my mom?* (Mom: You can't just write about my life. You need something else.)
- She thinks *A Silent Treatment* needs a new silent treatment. (Mom: It's a good title.)
- She's not angry at me. (Mom: I was mad at myself and took it out on you.)
- She's angry at me because I've spent more time writing about her than I've spent with her. (Mom: *I was never too busy when you needed something.*)
- She's angry at me because I've spent more time with Chris than with her. (Mom: I know that's not right of me, but I miss when it was just us.)

Should I have started, as I once did, with her first memory? Her great-grandfather's fingers stiffened around her, and her great-grandmother said: Somebody grab Barbara.

He died holding her.

Should I write about her life before I was born? Because that's how her silence makes me feel: as if I don't exist.

If the daughter reconstructed the first forty-one years of her mother's life—before the daughter existed—this would also be a book about the daughter, because the mother's silence makes the daughter feel as if she, the daughter, does not exist, as if she might never, as if she never should have.

What happened to contractions? The forced profundity of *does not*.

The forced profundity, period.

There are too many possibilities, and I need to choose one.

I don't always know what's a weed.

Think of manageable tasks.

The MAINT REQD light probably means the car needs an oil change. I drive to a Jiffy Lube, and a mechanic says it will be done *in a jiffy*. He asks for my name. (Mom: I wish your father hadn't named you after me. He thought he was doing something sweet. He looked hurt when I told him I wished he hadn't done that. So I left the birth certificate as it was. But I insisted we call you Jeannie like we'd planned.)

Barbara, I tell him.

How do you spell that?

B-a-r-b—

A barbed wire tattoo wraps around his neck.

Don't know how to spell your name? he asks and laughs. I'm just teasing.

I go by Jeannie. I figure you need my legal name.

You're complicated, he says.

He tells me he's listing an address for me in Texas.

This is to protect you, he explains.

Oh, okay.

I sit in the waiting area. Barb/barbed. A barbed wire is used for protection. My mom's silence, like barbed wire, keeps me out, protects her. Does she believe it protects me from her, from words she might regret? But then, there are her letters to consider. (Mom: *We never did get along.*)

When the mechanic hands me my keys, I almost ask: Why Texas?

But I like the mystery.

I park in the alley behind our house. My mom usually walks Max around this time. I drive around the block and park in front of our house. But if she assumes I'm parked in the alley, where I normally park, she'll use our front gate to avoid me. I drive back to the alley and park.

I open the car door.

I close the car door.

I google *what do you do if your mother shows you the silent treatment?*

Someone suggests *enjoy the peace and quiet.*

I'm not a mother, have no desire to be a mother, but I feel offended on behalf of mothers.

(Mom: I always wanted a daughter.)

A year after she moved in, I asked Chris if he wanted children.

The question, he said, is do you want children?

A kid would give my mom something to do. A sense of purpose.

That is not a reason, he said, to have children.

(Mom: I used to get so jealous of women who had daughters.)

Only when I was a child pushing a plastic baby in a plastic stroller did I want to be a mother. I circled pictures of cribs in catalogues, listed names I'd choose: Josephina, Gabriella, Isabella, Aurora. (I assumed I'd have girls.)

When I stopped playing with dolls, I stopped wanting children. But I've wanted, for as long as I can remember, to be a good daughter.

After my dad died, I began writing a book to demonstrate my love for him. I finished it a decade later, then told my mom I'd write another book, a book for her, and she said: You have to do things for yourself.

Before the book was published, she asked if there'd be a dedication page.

The book is the dedication, I said. It starts as a book for Dad but turns into a book for you.

Oh okay, she said quietly.

I didn't tell her that when I asked my publisher for a dedication page, it was too late.

I bought this house hoping she'd see our new arrangement as a greater dedication of love. But I hadn't thought through all the responsibilities and expectations: hers and mine. Since she moved in, I've felt pressured to demonstrate my love every day. If a day passes without my spending time with her, I consider myself a terrible daughter.

The reason I'm not a mother: I've thought through the responsibilities and expectations, and I doubt I could fulfill them. Daughtering is hard enough.

I dash from the car, through the yard, to the back door, through the kitchen, the dining room, the living room, and up to my office. I stare at the photo framed on my desk.

It shows my mom and me on a park bench in downtown Sandusky the day of my second ballet recital. I'm holding a sign with JEANNIE stenciled on it, and she's smiling wide. I'm five years old. I'm wearing a yellow camisole and tutu dress with gold-sequined trim, white tights, white ballet slippers, and white feathers in my brown hair. She's wearing small hoop earrings, a matching gold necklace, jeans, and a white V-neck top with sleeves that come to her elbows. Her hair, thick and ash blonde, is parted to the side and falls at her shoulders. Her big sunglasses hide her blue eyes. Her right arm is wrapped around me, holding me close. My jacket is on her lap. She's beautiful.

I remember that day: my mom applying my lipstick, or maybe just tinted lip balm, and powdering my skin. I remember my dad brushing my hair and securing it into a bun. I remember carefully stenciling my name on the sign and adding glitter to each letter. I didn't yet know that my real name was Barbara Jean, the same as hers. I didn't yet know that he'd die, and she'd stop speaking to me—and that her silence, like his death, would cause me to question what kind of daughter I was.

THE NEXT DAY

ONE OF US SHOULD GO DOWN THERE, CHRIS SAYS.

It's locked, I tell him.

I have the key.

We should respect her privacy.

Given her age, he says, it's not unreasonable to want to check on her.

She's fine. I saw her take out her trash this morning.

Do you want my mom to call her?

We'll probably just hear New York, New York.

The longer this goes—

I know, I say, but I think we should wait for a sign that she's ready.

If you want me to go down there, he says.

No, it should be me. She takes Max for a walk soon. If I don't see them leave, I'll go down there.

It's up to you, he says.

Can you put the wind chime back? I ask.

Signs my mom wants to end the silence:
- She reads on the deck—usually in the chair facing the dining room windows.

- She reads on the front porch—usually in the chair closest to the door.
- She moves my clothes from the washer to the dryer. She folds them and carries them to the dining room when Chris and I are gone or asleep.

I watch YouTube videos about the silent treatment. A licensed psychologist firmly instructs:
1. Don't apologize. (Mom: *Don't ask me to forgive you.*)
2. Don't respond with the silent treatment. (Mom: Don't talk to me.)
3. Don't engage at all. (Mom: Don't even look at me.)

The psychologist says: When you highlight how their actions impact you, they'll keep doing it to remain in control. The more out of control you appear to be, the more in control they feel.

But by not engaging *at all*, I'm waiting for her, and doesn't that give her control, and isn't control what she's after?

Maybe Chris is right.

One YouTuber says: There are two camps of people who use the silent treatment. The first are the active givers. These people are manipulators, abusers, narcissists. The second are the passive givers. These people are insecure. They perceive the silent treatment as dignified.

(Mom: We didn't want to say something we'd regret.)

Another YouTuber suggests using humor to end a silence.

A few years ago, I tried that. She was reading on the back deck, a sign she was ready for the silence to end. The pandemic was in its early days.

I guess social distancing is no fun, I said, when everybody's doing it.

She smiled, and I said: Please don't do this again.

I won't, she lied.

And there she goes, carrying Max.

(Mom: These animals are all I have. They keep me going.)

She moved here with two big dogs, Guido and Shu Shu. She'd had Shu Shu for almost sixteen years, and Guido for almost seventeen. Before Guido died, she repeated to him my dad's last words to her: You're my best friend.

I've had dogs all my life, she told me. I feel so lonely without one.

She said she wanted a small dog.

One I can carry up the stairs, she said, in case the dog gets arthritis.

Every week, for months and months, I refreshed shelter websites and submitted adoption applications to local rescues. My mom didn't know how to submit the online applications, nor did I want her to. Her emails resembled ransom notes. She didn't pay attention to caps lock.

Whenever a small dog's profile appeared on a shelter's website, it included the line: *I already have received the maximum number of applications.*

How, how, how? I'd shout at the computer.

Rescue organizations rejected my applications because we'd never crate-trained dogs. So I researched crate-training and applied to more rescue organizations. On phone interviews, they could tell I was lying. They told me dogs liked their crates. Finally, I snapped: I didn't know there'd been a survey.

Next, I arrived at shelters before they opened. Other people had the same idea. They were usually parents with children. I let them cut ahead of me—all except for the boy punching his dad's thigh, repeating: I want a dog.

I didn't tell my mom about all these trips. I didn't want her to get her hopes up.

So when Max's profile appeared—small, a history of peacefully coexisting with cats—I called the shelter and begged. No one else, they said, had applied for him. Maybe his age and his missing eye were off-putting.

He's perfect, my mom said.

He was ten. The average life expectancy for a shih tzu is ten to sixteen years.

Please, I whispered to him. We'll throw you the best sweet sixteen.

Jung calls, and our conversation begins the way it usually does: Why do we do this to ourselves?

Like me, she's writing her third book. Hers is fiction.

Anytime you want me to read pages, Jung says, I will.

I ask her if I can talk out an ethical question instead.

A mother inherently has so much power over a child, I say, but a writer has so much power over any person they're writing about. My fear is, Am I being fair enough? I worry this angle misrepresents her. But her silence is all I can think about.

As an observer to this process, Jung says, as opposed to a reader of the pages, I think you've been working really, really hard to write a book that is fair and that doesn't hurt your mom's feelings, but you're also talking about behavior that is deeply hurtful. I've been wondering if part of your frustration about finishing comes from the fact that the book is born out of love: You offered to do this for her because you love her, but you're also afraid of it.

She gave me permission to write about her silent treatment, I say, which is very selfless, and I worry she's letting me because she believes a mother should be selfless. What if she doesn't actually want me to write *A Silent Treatment*?

Isn't that an umbrella that covers this book? Jung asks. The worry that you're going to write it even with her permission and encouragement and she's going to be mad at you for it?

I wish *A Silent Treatment* was fiction. (Mom: I prefer memoirs. I like knowing that somebody actually went through the experience.)

> # THE NEXT DAY

LAST NIGHT I DREAMED SHE WAS MOVING OUT. Men loaded an old-fashioned car with stacks of cardboard boxes. Chris and I watched from our living room windows.

Do you want to say goodbye to her? Chris asked.

No, I said. She told me not to talk to her.

I woke up and almost asked Chris if she was gone, but then I remembered that the men had stuffed her bed, dresser, and love seat into the car's trunk. Impossible, I thought and returned to sleep.

I google *old-fashioned car*, and a Cadillac with big bullet-shaped fenders appears. It matches the car from my dream. Made in 1942, this model was discontinued on account of the war. My mom was born in 1942.

My mom was, appropriately enough, born into the Silent Generation—the McCarthy era, when speaking out could be cause for punishment—a coincidence I'm imagining is a sign that a book about her silent treatment can also be a book for and about her.

For and about.

It's the *for and about* I find daunting—yet why pursue a writing project that I believe I can complete easily? Or complete at all? (Mom: You're a perfectionist, just like your father. You sure don't take after me.)

But my compulsion to write about her silent treatment feels different from the desire to publish.

I almost wrote *punish*.

A couple of years ago, some months into her longest silence, I researched the silent treatment, hoping this might numb me from hers, or at least confirm that my pain made sense. I remember a peer-reviewed study claiming that social exclusion activates the same area of a victim's brain that physical abuse activates. I believe it, but I say this as someone who's never been beaten. Unlike my mom.

It's a wonder I made it out of my childhood alive, she prefaced stories about her mother's cruelty.

There was the time her mother threw a knife at her, the time her mother threw a rake at her, the time her mother hit her because my mom had stabbed her mother's boyfriend—just his hand, though, when she was twelve, because he'd tried to get into bed with her. (My mom slept with a knife under her pillow.) After my mom explained why she'd stabbed him, her mother refused to believe her.

I don't know why she hated me, my mom told me. I never asked her.

I know my mom loves me, but I don't know why, since moving here, she has repeatedly punished me, off and on, with silence.

(Mom: I don't know why I do it.)

I don't know if I can do this, I tell Sarah.

Sarah and I talk every week. She's an actor and writer in New York. We became friends in graduate school more than a decade ago and have swapped writing ever since. For a year now, she's been asking to read pages, and each time I say: Soon.

Every time you talk about this project, Sarah says, the question I keep hearing is, What do we owe our parents? And what do you owe her specifically, and it's so interesting that you set it up for yourself.

You mean because I promised her a book and now I have to write it?

Exactly. Which is a much more concrete version of this question: What do we owe our parents? What you seem to be negotiating is, How do I be me and have my own life and still be a dutiful daughter? Which is much more important to you than to other people, just so you know.

More important to me?

Yes. Often people just say, The relationship I have with my parents is the relationship that I have—where we're all people and we're doing the best we can—rather than raking themselves over the coals the way you do. So much of the conflict that you have about writing this is whether you're being a good daughter. You question what you're allowed to say. And it all goes along with the silent treatment. And so maybe at some point you want to explore why that is such a big deal for you.

I think of my mom's mother throwing a rake. (Mom: It stuck in my face. She wouldn't take me to the hospital because she knew she'd get in trouble. I still have the scar. My mother had no control of her emotions.)

Does my mom believe she's controlling her emotions through silence?

If I bring that rake into the raking-over-the-coals metaphor, I am saying what exactly? I'm scarred by my mom's anger like she was scarred by her mother's? (Mom: My mother beat us kids for the smallest thing. You have no idea. She threw my dog against the wall, and he started having seizures. That's how cruel she was.)

She is, I believe, doing the best she can. She's certainly doing better than her mother. (Mom: I never wanted to be like my mother. Our house was filthy. Water bugs climbing out of the fridge. Dirty dishes stacked for days. I'd clean. My mother never cleaned. Never. I think that's why I care so much about things being clean and organized.)

But am I doing the best I can?

Organize yard tools.

My mom already organized our yard tools.
Why do we own three rakes?

A month ago, when I returned home from physical therapy for neck, shoulder, and back pain (probably caused, the therapist said, from so much time reading and writing), my mom was in the garage.

Do you and Chris want to keep this? she asked.

Filing crates, a coffee table, a Formica table, a shoe rack, an extra hose: I agreed to donate all of it. She lifted one side of the coffee table.

You get the other side, she said. We'll put it in the front yard. Somebody will take it.

It's pretty heavy, I said.

I can carry it, she insisted.

I hesitated. My neck and shoulders ached from dry needling.

I bet I can get it on my own, she continued.

No, no, I told her. Let me help.

Chris joins me in the garage. He's searching for a wrench.

No empty boxes yet, I tell him, but it's just started.

A sticker on our red moving dolly says *Salvador*. When we lived in Brooklyn, he bought a label maker.

What other stuff did you name? I ask.

That was a long time ago, he says nostalgically.

He goes to his enormous steel tool cabinet, a recent gift from my mom.

Wow, your mom organized everything.

He picks up a flat metal box, my dad's wrench kit, and opens it. Envelopes slip out.

This has never happened before, he says.

The felt liner, I tell him. My dad must have put those in the liner.

Do you—

Yes, I interrupt.

I spread the envelopes on my office floor. One is addressed to her father, another to her friend Karen. The handwriting matches my mom's. They're not stamped. Another envelope is blank on the outside.

I start with the blank one. Inside is a receipt for a poncho, a cosmetic bag, a soap dish, and a toothbrush holder. On the back: *Will you ask your husband if it would be better for me to file for separation or divorce. I don't care what happens to Terry. He has family in New York. I want to protect Jeannie. Ask him about the charges for the lawyers. This was my house. Do I have to pay him off to get him out?*

There's no *Dear So-and-So*. The receipt is dated August 8, 1995. I was eleven years old.

In the same envelope is a letter to someone named Betty. My mom used lined paper: *Since marrying Terry I have lost all my friends and relatives.*

All her friends?

All her relatives?

I haven't seen Dad for seven years.

My dad offered to build an addition on our house for her father.

(Mom: I didn't really want him there, but your dad was big on family. The old man was all excited about it, but his girlfriend said no. She didn't like kids. You probably don't remember this, but she tried to push you down the stairs. After that, we told him not to bring her over every day. We didn't say she couldn't come. We suggested he bring her on Sundays. We wanted to make sure she was never alone with you. But the old man said if she wasn't welcome, he wasn't welcome. He stopped talking to me after that.)

I never saw her father again. When he died seventeen years later, he left my mom a dollar in his will.

I haven't seen any of the family.

Betty must be a relative, the way my mom intimately references her family. *Dad*, not *my dad*; *any of the family*, not *any of my family*.

(Mom: In and out of jail all the time, they're bad news. I don't want them at the house.) We played hide-and-seek when the doorbell rang. (Mom: Hurry. Let's hide. Your dad is going to count to ten.) Only later, when I was older, did I learn that her siblings, Butch and Donna, or their children had been outside.

Donna stopped over Xmas and her husband seemed very nice.

So she did see family.

I wish I had some family to visit and I'd take my daughter and leave.

Did she want Betty to invite us to stay with her?

(Mom: Your dad wanted you to have family. One Thanksgiving he insisted we invite Butch and Donna and their kids. I told him, You don't know my family. But I went along with it. They came, and everything was F-this and F-that. Donna's son punched his wife. Later your dad said he should've listened. He thought I'd been exaggerating.)

If I walk out Jeannie will hate me so I have to put up with all the unhappiness.

She once asked me if I'd accept a divorce. I was ten or eleven. We were walking through town, just the two of us, as we often did when I was a child. It was spring or summer. I remember the stench of garbage. We were near the junkyard in our neighborhood. I said I wanted her to be happy. She said I could see my dad on weekends, and I said okay. We never discussed it again.

Oh well my mother always said: You make your bed, you sleep in it.

(Mom: My mother was a cruel and hateful woman. She never should have had kids.)

The only good thing that happened is my daughter. I feel so bad for Jeannie because she's such a bright child. Even she doesn't want her father around her friends. She loves him but I know she's ashamed of how he acts.

Ashamed?

Karen has been my friend for over twenty two years and he finally managed to ruin that.

Karen's grandson bullied me. (Mom: He slammed a door on your hand, and Karen said that was just how kids played. He'd been mean before, but he really hurt you. Your dad and I didn't want you over there after that. Your dad suggested I have Karen come to our house instead, but she'd always bring her grandson. It just got too hard.)

When Karen's son overdosed, my dad sped over and gave him mouth-to-mouth. (Mom: Your dad told me he knew her son was dead already, but he kept trying. He didn't know how to deliver the news.)

I open the envelope addressed to Karen. My mom wrote on yellow legal paper: *I love you like a sister and I want you to know no matter where I end up you'll always be my best friend. You didn't do anything wrong. I did! I married a man old enough to be my father! Why I didn't listen to people I'll never know. I only know I love my daughter more than life itself. Even Jeannie is afraid of him.*

Afraid?

Jeannie doesn't want her father to even go to school because she's ashamed of how he acts.

Ashamed, again?

I can no longer live this way and I've decided I need to get out. I know how much it will hurt Jeannie but I need to get out. I hope to let you know where we're at but hope you will keep it to yourself. Terry judges people and according to him no one is any good.

My dad could be bluntly judgmental about others. He once told the owner of a local Italian restaurant: You expect people to eat here when you're picking your nose in front of everybody?

My mom grabbed my hand and said, We're going.

In the car, she told him: Why do you have to do that? Why do you have to embarrass us?

Later she laughed about it. (Mom: People always knew where they stood with your dad.)

I felt it better to stay away than to let you be subjected to his evil.

Evil?

He's ruined everything he touches.

Chris knocks.

She wrote horrible things, I tell him. She called my dad evil. She claimed I was afraid of him. Do you think he believed that?

Of course not, Chris says. Think of her letters to you. When she's mad, this is what she does.

The envelopes aren't stamped. It's not like he took them out of the mailbox. I don't think so anyway.

She probably handed them to your dad and asked him to put stamps on them.

But what about the blank envelopes?

Remember when the boiler was acting up? Chris asks.

Vaguely, I say.

She wasn't talking to us, he says, so you texted her that I needed to look at it. And when I went down there, there was a letter on the countertop. She wrote to a friend of hers that I didn't do anything around the house.

I'm sorry, I tell him.

It's not your fault, he says. When she's not in one of her moods, she's great.

(Mom: *I can no longer live this way and I've decided I need to get out.*)

I need to get out. Go for a drive.

The weed is still in the passenger seat. I throw it over our fence.

(Mom: Your dad could be possessive. It drove me nuts. He used to look at his watch before I went to the grocery store. I knew he was timing me.)

Groceries, now there's a productive errand. I choose a store not within easy walking distance.

An egg carton advertises *happy hens*. I check for broken shells.

When did eggs start coming with newsletters?

When the barn doors open, the hens dash outside to bathe in fresh air and sunshine—some solo, some in small clusters, some taking their own sweet time, and some preferring to stay inside.

How nice it'd be to dash outside without first peeking out my windows.

I put the eggs back on the shelf.

The carton calls them *ethical*.

Oh fine.

I move them to my cart, these plenary indulgences for the Anthropocene.

In front of me, at checkout, a girl of maybe five or six pulls her mother's arm, says: Take your hand off.

The mother asks why, and the girl says: I want to keep it.

But then I wouldn't have a hand, the mother says.

So? the girl asks.

Hang a sharp right, and I see the psych hospital. A student called me from there a year ago.

It's boring here, she told me. You said your hospital stays were boring.

I did? I asked.

She clarified: I mean that you *wrote* that they were boring. In your memoir. The first one.

Said and *wrote* are often used interchangeably. If only writing were as easy as speaking.

(Mom: Talk is cheap. Don't believe someone unless they put it in writing.)

I park outside the hospital, open the carton. The newsletter features henkus, haikus about hens.

Beneath the shade trees
Gentle clucking from the deep
As hens tell stories

If I recite the henku casually to a nurse or doctor, maybe they'll let me live here for a while.

Using my phone, I google *plenary indulgence*. A Catholic church website defines it as a special indulgence that, if all requirements are met, eliminates temporal punishment for one's sin.
 If I finish the book—
 If I dedicate it to her—
 But a book exploring her silences— (Mom: You're the writer. Write what you want to write. Don't worry about me.)
 Is *plenary indulgences for the Anthropocene* too clever and/or clunky?

The is-it-poetic test that I use with students: If you say the sentence casually to a friend, will they think you're losing it?

A rake is leaning against a tree on the hospital grounds.

Interpreting coincidences as signs is a symptom of mania.

Grandiosity, another.

Thinking of my mom's letters to me, I feel far from grandiose. (Mom: *I never wanted to admit how selfish you are.*)

Her letters about my dad—

Finding them now—

(Mom: *He's ruined everything he touches.*)

Dad?

Your mom just needs time to cool off, he used to say.

(Mom: *Even Jeannie is afraid of him.*)

One month before my college graduation, I was hospitalized for a mixed dysphoric state. The doctors and nurses repeatedly suggested I call my mom.

She can't know where I am, I said.

But she's your mom, they said.

She's still grieving my dad, I explained.

I didn't want to worry her, I told a therapist years later. I was trying to protect her.

Do you think, he asked, you were trying to protect yourself?

I don't follow.

I've known you for a long time now, he said. I've heard you talk about your mom, about the way she sometimes reacts to difficult situations.

I'm okay. I'm okay. I'm okay. (Mom: You know you can always talk to me.) Really, I'm okay.

We were at the cemetery office, paging through a binder of gravestone options.

You take care of it, she said and abruptly returned to the car.

(Mom: *I know she's ashamed of how he acts.*)

Some months after my dad's funeral, I told her I wanted to break up with my boyfriend, and she snapped: At least you have someone.

(Mom: You have to write about the bad stuff.)

A year after his funeral, I started to tell her I'd been sexually assaulted: Something happened at the party—

Well, she interrupted, were you drinking?

She was cleaning what used to be the living room. My dad died there in a bed borrowed from hospice.

She glared. She'd never glared at me. Growing up, I could tell her when someone had hurt me, and she would comfort me and take my side—even when I pointed out why I deserved some of the blame. (Mom: You always look for the good in people. You forgive too easily.)

She returned to cleaning.

I eventually told her the full story of the assault. I didn't want her to learn about it when strangers did. My book about it would soon be sent to reviewers. This was almost four years ago.

You did drink a lot, she said and started crying.

I'm okay, I said.

You're not a mother, she told me. You don't know what it's like.

I sat as still and straight as possible, as I had when she threw herself over his coffin.

Afterward I bought train tickets for us to New York. I hoped the trip would distract her.

I wasn't there for you after your dad died, she said years and years later.

Yes, you were, I told her.

No, she said. I wasn't.

But I didn't let her be.

It's easy to consider the good in people if you were raised by people who loved you and were gentle toward you. (Mom: Me, I hold grudges. I can't help it. I'm still mad at those girls who were mean to you in grade school.)

You're complicated, the mechanic said.

Take your hand off, the girl told her mother.

A hand is a limb. A tree has a limb. Family tree. That rake is leaning against a tree.

Using my phone, I google *rake over the coals*. In medieval times, Catholics dragged and raked heretics over hot coals. Nobody told me that in Catholic school.

But the coals are what, in this metaphor?

Last month I dropped her off at Kohl's, drove home, moved some sentences around in an old draft, and returned after she texted an hour or so later. I should have asked if I could join her, but no, I came home and accomplished nothing. I raked myself over the coals for not shopping with her at Kohl's.

Am I making this too complicated?
 What am I even making?
 Besides mixed metaphors.

I call Sarah and describe the letters.

I can't remember ever feeling afraid or ashamed of my

dad, I say. And he wasn't evil. He wasn't perfect, but he wasn't evil. Just that word: *evil*.

Are you going to write about them? she asks.

I don't know. I want to ask her for permission.

You're going to tell her?

I can't write about them otherwise.

You can always write about them, she says, and remove those passages later.

(Mom: Throw it away.)

With my plenary indulgences for the Anthropocene, I drive back home.

Back home, when my mom says it, almost always means Sandusky.

2 A.M.

WIPER FLUID, I FORGOT WIPER FLUID.

3:30 A.M.

WHY DID HE SAVE THE LETTERS?

I open the envelope addressed to her father. She wrote on lined white paper. Its creases have yellowed.

You probably won't hear from me anymore but thought I'd give you an explanation. I've taken Jeannie and left Sandusky. Its to dangerous for Jeannie and I anymore. I can no longer live with Terry.

Dangerous?

Once I leave, I'll never come back.

But she claimed to have already left.

I think Terry has a past life with the mafia so I'm leaving.

(Mom: Your dad was a loan shark when he lived in New York. When the Mafia learned he was leaving, they asked him for his ledger. So he threw it in the water. He knew what the Mafia would do to those people. He was broke by the time I met him. I had more money than he did, and that's not saying much.)

After he died, we received a letter from a stranger: *When I tried to repay him, he wouldn't accept it. A lot of people owed him money, but I don't think he ever got it back. He was very decent.*

Maybe not a loan shark then.

I'm going to head for Michigan. Contact Karen and she'll get you information.

Why Michigan?

A poncho, a cosmetic bag, a soap dish, and a toothbrush holder might appear on a packing checklist. Was the receipt a prop?

I've known a long time how I made a mistake but I wanted Jeannie to have a family. I'm so ashamed that I could have been so stupid. I guess I really disappointed you but not as much as I've hurt myself.

Did she even plan to mail this?

(Mom: My father was never any help. He knew how bad my mother was, but he did nothing. When he died, I felt nothing.)

Was my dad her intended reader? Or did she write these letters strictly for herself?

Did he ruminate over them? Reflect? Did he take her at her word?

(Mom: Your dad's sister Anna told him, I'm so glad you're with Barbara. She's so kind. And your dad laughed. He said, You come live here and see her when she's mad. The pope could be in front of her and it wouldn't matter.)

I believed her when she called me *such a disappointment*. I believed her when she called me *selfish*.

(Mom: I didn't mean any of that.)

Her dialogue goes in parentheses—when? When it's intrusive? (Mom: *You are such a disappointment.*) And when does it deserve its own line?

(Mom: After your dad died, I went nuts. He was gone, and you were at college, and I felt so alone. I should have been there for you.)

Maybe it should be unpredictable, like her silences. (Mom: It's your book.)

It's the book's structure, I told her, that's especially tough to figure out. I might set it during your longest silence.
 That's a good idea, she said.
 I just need some kind of narrative arc, a through line.

Write it however it needs to be written, she said.

Calling it *her* dialogue seems inaccurate. I'm selecting and arranging it—
And do excerpts from her letters count as dialogue?

(Mom: Write it however it needs to be written.)

Did she hide the letters? (Mom: *I don't care what happens to Terry.*) But why behind the liner of his wrench kit? (Mom: What I wouldn't give to have him back.)

Did she ever write a letter addressed to my dad? Or was her silence more consuming?

A familiar question in writing workshops: Who is the intended audience?

When I return to bed, Chris opens his eyes.
I'm thinking, I tell him, that maybe I should be grateful for this silence. I forgot how horrible the silent treatment feels. Writing from within a silence is truer than reconstructing it. Perspective isn't true because we never have

perspective. The moment that we're experiencing is the truest thing.

You should write that down, he says.

That's why I get so frustrated, I continue, when people think memoir is strictly about the past. We tell stories about the past to make sense of why we feel or think the way we do. But we don't really know anything.

Have you slept?

TWO DAYS LATER

NOTE CARDS SEEMED LIKE A SMART IDEA yesterday.
- *Figurines with magnets on the bottom and you moved them around a track with a magnetic wand*
- *ATM self-checkout online banking ordering pet food*
- *10 yrs ago mattress salesman told me box springs were a scam and I told my mom and did that upset her because she'd been stressing the importance of getting a good box spring—I would've bought anything he recommended but he didn't recommend anything*

I crumple the note cards.

I scroll through the archives of my favorite podcast. I remember when the host interviewed me.
 You wrote your first book for over a decade, he said. You wrote your second book in eight months. So I'm assuming your third book is coming out in six weeks because you're getting quicker and quicker.
 We laughed.

Three years ago, that was.

I open the transcript. (Mom: *I never wanted to admit how selfish you are.*)

When I feel really stuck, I told him, I just open the refrigerator and I stare into it as if the answer is there. So much of the writing process is just sitting and thinking and reading and it's not like you see in the movies, or like Philip Glass music is playing in the background and somebody's writing furiously. It's like going and getting a snack every twenty minutes, at least for me, that's what the writing process looks like.

So the refrigerator is key, he said.

The refrigerator is key, I said.

(Mom: *When I had to go home to clean it was awful. You gagged when you opened the refrigerator.*)

I open the refrigerator. Our hot sauce bottles are clumped with jam jars and syrup. And how did our ketchup find its way next to our salad dressing? I had a system. (Mom: You're just like your dad. You get real worked up over small things.)

Is this disarray of condiments metaphorical?

Am I not letting the story go where it needs to go? (Mom: A book needs conflict.)

Am I trying to control it too much? (Mom: Write the book you want to write.)

Am I trying to control my emotions by controlling the book? (Mom: My mother had no control of her emotions.)

(Mom: Your dad and I couldn't figure out why you put so much pressure on yourself.)

Other children often told me: My parents say it's wrong that your parents had you. They say your dad is too old.

My behavior, I believed, reflected their parenting. If I was perfect, they were perfect.

(Mom: We weren't perfect.)

I call Sarah and summarize my realization: If I question their parenting, or if I'm not the perfect daughter, I'm supporting this idea that I shouldn't have been born. I've been defending my existence, which sounds so dramatic, but I think it's true.

In order, Sarah says, to come down on the side that, yes, you should have been born, that means your parents had to have been perfect. They couldn't have done anything wrong because if they did anything wrong then you shouldn't have been born. That's kind of what you're saying. And then if you weren't perfect, also you shouldn't have been born. So you're representing. Questioning their parenting is going on the side of the people who said you shouldn't have been born. It's an all-or-nothing thing. They have to be one hundred percent perfect or they shouldn't have been parents. It's not like they could have been human parents.

And now I don't need therapy ever again, I tell her. Thank you.

A local but otherwise unfamiliar number. Hesitantly, I answer the phone.

I'm with Advanced Radiology, a woman says. Can I speak with Barbara Vanasco?

I'm her daughter.

This is for X-rays. Says here they're for ongoing neck problems.

Oh right, I say. Those are for me.

They're for Barbara Vanasco.

My mom and I technically share a name.

So you are Barbara?

I go by Jeannie, but my legal name is Barbara.

We schedule the appointment.

Wait, the woman says, this is odd. Your phone number and email address are linked to your mom's charts.

I explain: I schedule my mom's appointments because she doesn't trust herself to drive very far, isn't great with email, and sometimes has trouble hearing the phone.

Your home address is also linked, the woman says. Is that a mistake?

ANOTHER TWO DAYS LATER

I OPEN THE VIDEO SOFTWARE THAT MY PSYCHIatrist uses. A pop-up box assures me that her office takes my privacy seriously. I have two memoirs and however many personal essays to my name.

I drag her face right beneath my camera. In my hospital records, doctors noted my lack of eye contact.

My psychiatrist looks like she's looking out my window, to the right of me, but really she's looking at me. Is my attempt at eye contact now concerning?

I ask for more clonazepam.

You don't normally go through it this quickly, she says.

It's my mom, I say.

Again? she asks.

ONE WEEK LATER

SOME DAYS I THINK TODAY IS YESTERDAY, OR yesterday hasn't happened, or tomorrow is today.

A cricket leg floats in the cats' drinking fountain. The other day, a different leg was in the empty tub.

Am I living with the Mafia? I ask Kiffawiffick. Where are the rest of the bodies?

I feel my hair. (Mom: What about the United States government? Is what the mob does any worse?)

I sit at the dining room table and pull back the left drape slightly.

The stairwell is dark. The sky is dark.

Maybe she's asleep.

I go to the kitchen and start brewing coffee. The stove's clock reads 6:44.

When I return to the dining room, the deck lights have detected motion, brightening the drapes. I peek through the tiny gap between them. She's carrying a bag into the alley. Did she hear my footsteps above her moments ago? Did she deliberately leave her apartment when I left this room?

Using my phone, I google *what time is sunrise in Baltimore*.

6:54.

She's cutting it close.

Do I smell cinnamon? Is she burning scented candles?

Her door is locked.

What if there's an emergency, I asked her, and rescuers need to reach you?

I won't leave without my animals, she said. Let me die if I don't have the animals.

I google *scented candle starts fire*.

Her outside door slams.

Sometimes it gets stuck.

No use testing the smoke alarm. She'd probably stay down there to prove a point.

Upstairs: two fire ladders, three cat carriers, one fireproof rope to lower the carriers, three fireproof bags intended for babies or pets, two fire blankets, a fire extinguisher.

Downstairs: two fire extinguishers, three cat carriers, one fire blanket, two bottles of spray for small fires.

My mom's apartment: one cat carrier, one fire extinguisher, one bottle of spray for small fires, one fire blanket.

Why are you so worried about fires? friends have asked.

I also worry about other things.

Chris once explained that if her smoke alarm went off, ours would too.

They talk to each other, he said.

So our smoke alarms are on speaking terms.

New Year's Eve three years ago, Chris and I were in the car, on our way to dinner and a movie, when I asked him if I'd blown out the candle on our dining room table. Why I chose that night to light a candle, I have no idea. I rarely use candles. He said yes, but I called my mom's cell anyway, asked if she could check.

Sure, she said.

I thanked her, said I loved her, and she hung up.

She didn't say *I love you* back, I told him.

Maybe she didn't hear you, he said.

When we returned home, a letter was on the kitchen counter with the iPad I'd given her for Christmas. Stuck to the iPad was a Post-it that read, *I don't want anything from you.*

Chris hurried to the door off our dining room, which was locked, then hurried to the stairs off our deck. I suddenly understood: If you live with somebody, and you leave them a letter—

I gripped the kitchen counter.

When he returned, he said she was on her couch.

She let you in?

No, I could see her through the window in her stairwell. Do you want me to read the letter?

I nodded yes.

He read it to himself and said, I don't think you should read it.

He texted her: *I haven't shown the letter to Jeannie. I think you might regret it. Do you want me to throw it away?*

She probably felt left out, he said, because we celebrated New Year's without her.

Her television turns on, and the president says, C'mon, man.

I switch the air purifier to the loudest setting and take out the trash. Maybe twenty pairs of her shoes are in a laundry bag in our alley garbage can. Low-heeled dress shoes.

Trash pickup happened yesterday.

Donate Mom's props.

I should organize my closets.

But she wanted to help organize my closets.

Do I wait for her?

In our coat closet is a framed poster of Nicolas Cage. A reprint from the American Library Association's READ campaign, it used to hang in our dining room. Cage is in a baggy gray sweater, leaning against a tree, holding Hermann Hesse's *Siddhartha*. I bought the poster because it reminded me of reading aimlessly in the Sandusky Library while my parents read nearby. Nicolas Cage was beside the point, as was *Siddhartha*, which happens to be upside down. When friends laughed at this, I said: And you always hold your books right side up?

The first time my mom saw the poster, she said she never liked him.

As a person, I asked, or an actor?

An actor. He's not very good.

He actually has a lot of range, I said. Have you seen *Pig* or *Adaptation*? *Raising Arizona*? What about *Moonstruck*? You said you loved *Moonstruck*.

Moonstruck was good. He's not very good-looking, though, is he?

If you saw him in real life, you'd probably think he was really handsome.

I don't think so, she said.

And now I'm remembering when she said Al Pacino hadn't aged well.

He aged, I said. You've seen him act since he was young.

Robert De Niro hasn't aged very well either, she said.

Oh my god, I said. We all age. Just because you've aged well doesn't mean everybody gets to.

She's often mistaken for being twenty years younger than she is. A doctor recently told her whatever she was doing, she should keep it up.

The walking, I almost clarified. Not the silences.

Can't you see the stress lines on her forehead? a colleague recently said of me and laughed.

I was in a committee meeting when a much nicer colleague had asked if I was still advising a student group.

They're doing an amazing job, she'd said, to which he delivered his stress-lines line.

He'd made mean, petty comments before, but never about my appearance, and never in front of colleagues.

The nice colleague looked horrified. I don't know how I looked.

Old, I guess.

Which is why I'm now wearing these clip-on bangs around the house. I've taken scissors to cheap wigs, adding bangs to them in different styles, but these clip-ons seem the most realistic.

You don't have lines on your forehead, Chris told me.

This is why, I said, I don't share work in progress with you.

It's just getting old, I told a friend. People underestimate Nicolas Cage's craft.

I'm joking about him not reading, she said.

This photo shoot, I said, was probably one of many things he had to do in a single day. I bet the photographer instructed him to hold *Siddhartha* upside down. Because holding it right side up would make the scene look too posed.

You're getting kind of weird about Nicolas Cage, this friend said.

However many weeks ago, Chris, some strangers, and I took a ghost tour around New Orleans. After the guide pointed out Cage's former house, she mocked him for going into debt and criticized his acting. The strangers on the tour laughed.

I almost said: The real estate market collapsed. He could have declared bankruptcy, but he didn't. Instead, he accepted a bunch of bad roles, and he gave his all to every one of them. That is the sign of a real professional. Also, how does this connect with ghosts?

Where did I read that bangs are a sign of an approaching nervous breakdown?

After New Orleans, I removed the poster from the wall.

I'm okay. This closet is okay. All the closets are probably okay. But my mom—

I should have taken her to New Orleans instead of Chris.

Organize closets, really? Can't I figure out a more exciting mother-daughter activity?

A friend texts a few of us about happy hour drinks. *YES!!!!!* I reply.

(Mom: I am so friggin bored.)

After moving in, she regularly asked for tasks. First, I told her to reorganize the books. Chris wanted the poetry books separate from fiction and nonfiction because most poetry collections could easily disappear among the bigger books.
    Is this poetry or fiction or nonfiction? she asked.
    I said that if she started reading it, and it seemed very confusing or had a lot of blank space, to put it in a separate pile.

What do I do with plays? she asked.

What do I do with books about poetry? she asked.

What do I do with biographies of writers? she asked.

What do I do with authors' letters or diaries? she asked.

I told her to use her judgment, that it actually wasn't a big deal.

What now? she asked a couple of days later.

That task, I had thought, would take a week. She'd organized well over a thousand books.

Let me think, I said.

A day later, she asked: Do you have anything for me to do?

I suggested she stain all the bookshelves mounted to the walls. She'd need to do this outside.

It's nice out, she said. It's a good time to do this.

She stacked the books around our downstairs, and Chris removed the shelves.

I can carry them, she told us.

Please, I said, just let us help you move them.

After she finished and we remounted the shelves, my mom put the books back.

What next? she asked.

I told her to shelve all the books together, regardless of genre.

But doesn't Chris want the poetry separate?

He's fine with it, I lied. I told him we have too many books that span multiple genres.

What now? she asked.

I'm losing my mind, I told Chris one night.

He said: The backyard needs to be mulched. That's hard work, though.

Perfect, I said.

So the next day, Chris ordered mulch to be delivered.

You don't have to do it, he emphasized to her.

I can do it, she said.

Do a little bit each day, he said.

Okay, she said.

She finished the yard the same day the mulch arrived.

I see where you get it from, Chris said.

(Mom: I have to earn my keep.)

But I wanted her to enjoy herself, and I wanted her to make friends. With her permission:
- I organized a book club, one with women her age, that met at a restaurant down the street from our house. She went to one meeting. (Mom: If they want to do their book club, they can do it without me.)
- I filled out and submitted her application to volunteer at an animal shelter. She went to orientation. (Mom: I'm not volunteering there. I'm not going to risk bringing diseases back to my pets.)
- I enrolled her in continuing education classes for seniors, which met at a church in our neighborhood. She attended eight weeks of classes. (Mom: The people are all snobby, talking about their vacation homes and kitchen renovations.)

- I could see her points about the animal shelter and classes, but I also signed her up for continuing education classes at the university where I teach. Why those disappointed her, I forget.

(Mom: Tell them that you did try to help me.)

Have you noticed, a friend said, that nothing ever works out for your mom?

(Mom: But they've got it all wrong.)

Her outside door opens. I tense up, stare straight ahead at the bookshelves. The spines look blurry. My spine, when are my X-rays?
Will *A Silent Treatment* ever exist?
How often I forget to write down the right things.
She appears in a gap between the drapes, carrying Max. (Mom: These animals are all I have.)
I hurry to my bedroom, pile my dirty clothes in a laundry basket, and return to the dining room. To come and go from her apartment, she walks through the laundry room. This layout allows Chris and me to wash our clothes without bothering her. (Mom: You can always come through the apartment. I don't mind.) All I have to do is throw stuff in a machine and press a button.

But what if she's taking Max only into the yard?
She wouldn't do that, though. He doesn't like the mulch.
She could keep his walk short.

If they return when I'm in the laundry room, what would I say to her? I love you. Or is *I love you* insufficient? (Mom: Talk is cheap.)

I'm writing a book because nothing I say or do seems sufficient.

I'm on my laptop, shopping for underwear.
You still have to wash it, Chris says.
I was planning to wash it, I lie. In the bathtub.
Then I think: Why not wash my clothes in the bathtub?
He looks at the laundry basket at my feet.
I'll do your laundry, he says.
No, I should do it, I tell him. This is ridiculous. She's the one avoiding me.

I carry my dirty clothes to the bottom of the outside stairwell. I size up the door like it's looking for a fight. (Mom: Don't talk to me. Don't even look at me.)

I'm too sober for this.

I return to the table, part the drapes, and open the windows. I text my friends: *4pm happy hour???*

Should I return her dress shoes to the trash? Maybe she plans to retrieve them.

I open my laptop again. My cursor lingers over my computer's trash can, but I can't bring myself to empty it. How many *A Silent Treatment* files have I dragged into it?

(Mom: Throw it away.)

My friends reply with animated memes: sitcom characters dancing.

How did they do that?

GIFs, they're GIFs.

Jiffs like the *jiff* in Jiffy Lube, or is the *g* hard?

Everything seems so hard. (Mom: Sometimes I can't pronounce words because I had so many ear infections. I was taller than the other kids so I always got put in the back of the classroom. I couldn't hear the teacher.)

The other day, my students talked about stories on Instagram, and I said: Like flash fiction?

They laughed.

One of them said, She doesn't know what a story is.

(Mom: No wonder old people kill themselves.)

My leg is shaking, like a GIF.

I don't know what this story is.

Or I do, and I wish it were different.

Are parted drapes an invasion of her privacy?

I close the windows and drapes and move the table toward the middle of the room.

Is this entire project an invasion of her privacy?

(Mom: You have to write about the bad stuff.) (Mom: Your dad and I were soul mates.) (Mom: Throw it away.)

I take the approaching nervous breakdown off my forehead.

The bangs resemble a small animal.

(Mom: *I don't even know who you are anymore.*)

Over drinks, I tell friends how I'm preparing for bangs, and they laugh.

I explain, This way I know what it feels like to have hair on my forehead all the time.

One says, I feel like this says so much about you.

I must look embarrassed because she adds: It's not at all a bad thing. You really prepare.

But I'm putting more thought into getting bangs, I tell her, than I did to my mom moving in.

A couple of drinks later and, back home, a couple of drinks later, I'm feeling relaxed, like I could maybe do laundry.

If the door between the laundry room and my mom's living room is cracked open, as it sometimes is when she's ready to talk, I'll knock.

Mom? I'll ask.

If she doesn't answer, I'll toss my clothes into the washer and leave. Moving them to the dryer will become a middle-of-the-night operation. Removing them from the dryer will happen the next night. I'll need to wear one of our headlamps. Carrying the laundry basket and a flashlight is too hard, and sometimes the stairwell's motion-detecting light turns off too quickly.

But if she answers?

Maybe I should join an underwear of the month club.

Your mom left this for you, Chris says.

He's holding an envelope. My name is on it.

It was on the table on the deck, he says, under a rock. Do you want me to read it?

I nod yes, and he opens it.

Oh, he says.

What?

There's no letter. Just her copy of the car key, a bill for Max's food, and a check.

So an online pet pharmacy, I tell him, is the one thing keeping us in contact.

What if you take his food off autoship?

I can't, I say. She doesn't know how to use the online pharmacy. And anyway, his prescription is linked to my account.

She'd have to talk to you then, he says.

But what if she's too stubborn to ask for help?

So she'd call the vet's office, he says. She'd figure it out. She loves Max.

But then I'm being passive-aggressive.

She's the one ignoring you.

Do you think the key means she's moving? I ask.

Your mom is hard to figure out.

I can't take this coldness.

It's emotional abuse, he says.

I want to be careful, I say, about using the word *abuse*.

THE NEXT DAY

DOWN THE STREET FROM OUR HOUSE IS SOME kind of medical center. Its awning reads *Aphasia Life Enhancement*. I'm sitting on the steps where the regulars linger. Sometimes they ask how my day is, where I'm off to, but nobody's here today. I've never asked them if they recently regained the ability to understand or express speech, or if they treat people with aphasia. Maybe the center accepts patients with other illnesses. There's so much around me I don't know, and I don't know when knowing really matters, so I don't ask.

Just checking in, my editor texts. *How's it going?*

Across from the aphasia center was a women's-only gym until the pandemic closed it permanently.

I miss the text alerts: *A man will be in the gym between 3 and 5 p.m. today, performing maintenance.*

Some silences ago, I asked the receptionist if my mom had visited recently.

She's not speaking to me, I explained. If she hasn't used her membership the past few months, I'm wondering if I can stop payment until she returns.

Let me see what the computer will let me do, the receptionist said and started typing. It says here that you and your mom—

It's not a mistake, I said. Not in the way you're thinking.

I think I can finish it in a few months.

A year and four months ago, I texted that.

I don't know if I can write this, I tell Sarah.

I know I don't need to state the irony, she says.

What do you mean?

That in her giving you the silent treatment, you're silencing yourself.

I didn't think of that, I say. How did I not think of that?

I go to the cemetery a couple of blocks away. A dog is peeing on a headstone, and the dog's person looks at me apologetically. I smile, the person smiles, and it feels good to smile in a cemetery even if, buried at my feet, are an infant and her parents, or probably her parents. Same last name. Same year of death.

In grade school, I told God that when my parents died, I wanted to die with them. I asked if we could avoid house fires, car accidents, and tornadoes. Dying during sleep was preferable.

Is that okay? I asked a priest.

It's not normal, he said.

His response didn't seem normal—normal for a priest, I mean—which is probably why I remember it.

But what about it did he not consider normal?

The most memorable moments are the ones that stray from the ordinary, which is why I question this entire project.

A lot better! I text back.

(Mom: When I die, I don't want any fuss. I don't want a funeral or a showing. I don't want any announcement in the newspaper. Scatter my ashes over your dad's grave but do it at night. The cemetery charges a lot to open a grave. And only do it when you have the time.)

If one of you dies before the other, my mortgage lender told me, this could cause problems for the survivor. I'd legally change your name if I were you.

Just because we're going to share an address?

It's very hard, he said, to prove you're not dead after the government thinks you're dead.

But we have different Social Security numbers. And wouldn't they look at the birth dates?

I've seen it happen, he said.

You have?

I've heard of it happening.

So should I change my name before I buy the house?

You don't have enough time. But I'd do it. Eventually.

What would I choose for a middle name?

Jeannie Barbara sounds wrong.

Removing Barbara entirely—

(Mom: I wish your father hadn't named you after me. I knew it'd create problems.)

I could choose names that she wanted to give me. Isabella or Gabriella maybe. Gigi? She ended up naming one of our dogs Gigi. (Mom: That's what I wanted to name you, but your dad didn't like it.)

Or I could forgo a middle name altogether.

Terry J. Vanasco is on my dad's gravestone. I'm almost sure of it. The *J* stands for John. Giovanni Battista Vanasco, after John the Baptist, was his given name, same as his father's, but his Social Security card listed Terry J. Vanasco. The Social Security Administration asked him which name he preferred. (Mom: *I married a man old enough to be my father!*) When his father, a Sicilian immigrant, bought a barbershop, it was called Terry's. So rather than change the sign, his father started going by Terry, and my dad, still a boy, also became Terry.

(Mom: The Mafia used the barbershop's back room. You couldn't really say no to the Mafia, your dad said.)

(Mom: *I think Terry has a past life with the mafia so I'm leaving.*)

(Mom: Your dad wasn't in the mob. My ex-husband hired a private investigator and they didn't find anything. He was trying to sue me for the house. It was my house to begin with. And he wanted my statue of the Virgin Mary. Only thing my mother gave me. So we said, Fine, take the statue. We even paid him for half the house just to get the divorce over with. Even his lawyer thought he was out of his mind. His lawyer shook your dad's hand, said: I can tell you're a good man.)

You keep your dad young, doctors told me when I was a child. You give him energy.

How I interpreted this: Keeping my dad alive was my responsibility.

When I was in high school, he became housebound, and I believed I'd failed him. I hadn't spent enough time at home, and now he couldn't leave our home. I was too involved with drama club and yearbook and the school newspaper and Model UN and all the rest. I couldn't rest, didn't want to rest. Had I rested, I might have registered that he'd soon be *laid to rest*. A euphemism I hated.

1922–2002

What about the rest of his gravestone?

What do you want it to say? the cemetery worker asked.

My mom was waiting for me in the car. The *husband* should come first, I probably thought.

While you think, the cemetery worker said, do you want to pick out a fish for your mom? They make great company.

Small containers of blue, orange, and red betta fish cluttered her desk.

She has a dog, I said.

What about when her dog dies?

This seemed morbid, even for a cemetery worker.

But you can't put two betta fish together, she added. They'll kill each other.

Chris is in the dining room, eating breakfast.

These are really good eggs, he says. Did you see the newsletter?

If I die before you, I tell him, please don't bury me on top of my mom.

What? he asks.

And if she dies before me and I die before you, please don't bury her on top of me.

Let's think about happy things.

It's called a double-decker, I tell him.

Listen to this, he says and reads to me something about Clever Carla, the hen of the month.

Do you think the car key means she's moving? I ask.

I don't think she's moving, he says.

But you said we should think about happy things.

All day I feel guilty about my mean comment, but wouldn't moving make her happy? (Mom: *I'm going to get out of here as soon as I can.*)

Chris and I order takeout for dinner, and I realize: We drink coffee at the dining table but eat dinner at the coffee table. This observation, for some reason, seems profound.

We discuss what to stream.

No dystopian movies, I specify. And no possessed mothers.

We choose a show about an optimistic American football coach hired to manage a British soccer team. Chris asks me to raise the volume.

My mom might be asleep.

She can't hear our TV, he says.

That's what she says, I tell him.

Okay, put subtitles on.

I don't want to read, I say. Once they're on, I can't not see them.

If she can hear our TV, he says, she likely can hear us right now.

I turn up the volume.

Why do you think my dad saved the letters?

If he thought she was actually going to divorce him, Chris says, he might have thought they'd help him.

Help him?

Mothers usually get custody of the kids. I don't think he would have taken you from her. Maybe he thought this would mean shared custody.

But in the letters, I say, she claims it was dangerous for her and me to live with him.

Does she offer any examples?

No.

I love your mom, but when she's mad, she's like this whole other person.

His phone dings.

Food's ready, he says.

I'll go with you.

I stand on my toes, peering out the window on our back door. He looks out our dining room windows.

All clear, I say.

He drives. We turn right off our street, and the busy road becomes, in a matter of minutes, an avenue with a new name. I think of my mom's silent treatment. I'm moving straight along when suddenly, at some point, things shift. But when York becomes Greenmount, at least there's an unambiguous sign.

. . .

WHEN YOU PUT IT DOWN ON PAPER

A SMALL WHITE ORB-LOOKING THING, OUR NEW Google Home Mini sits next to our television. I don't like the Mini. (Mom: If I don't like somebody, they know it. I don't pretend.) But I have to talk to it if I want to adjust our downstairs lighting. Chris installed smart bulbs.

Hey Google. When are you listening?

I'm designed to wait in standby until I'm activated, like when you say: Hey Google.

Hey Google. What are some things I can do to relax?

Here is some information from the web that might possibly help. On the website health.clevelandclinic.org, they say: Baths create a good environment for meditation, thought, and escape—

Hey Google. Thank you. How do I take a relaxing bath?

On the website secretspa.co.uk, they say: Choose a favorite scented candle as well as a few other non-scented ones, and place these safely around the bathroom, and dim or switch off the lights.

Hey Google. How common are house fires in the United States?

On the website worthinsurance.com, they say: A home fire occurs every eighty-seven seconds.

Baths kind of disgust me, and I lack the thing that covers the drain. A stopper? But maybe a bath will help. I own two scented candles: the one I asked my mom to check on New Year's Eve three years ago and another, a gift from my friend Michelle. It was her mother's favorite scent, she told me. Even unlit, it smells nice: a blend of lime, basil, and mandarin. And its metallic lid fits the drain perfectly. I run warm water and pour in body wash. My makeshift stopper works. I get in the tub, close my eyes, and imagine low light from the candle's wick.

Every eighty-seven seconds?

But a tiny flame must be relaxing because why else risk a house fire?

Michelle's memoir is titled *Pure Flame*.

Michelle gave me the candle for supporting *Pure Flame*.

How am I only now processing the gift/title relevance?

In her memoir, Michelle explored her relationship with her mother. At the book launch last year, my mom sat in the front row. I served as a conversation partner.

Michelle told the audience: My mother referred to this as *our book*. She died before it came out.

During the Q&A, someone in the audience said: I'm not writing about my mother until she dies.

Others laughed. I glanced at my mom, gently shook my head no, as if to telepathically transmit: That is not what I'm doing.

What am I doing?

I towel off, dress, lie on my office daybed, and cry.

(Mom: I think you should write about it.)

Michelle also told the audience: When my editor asked me why I wanted to write this book, I said it was the hardest thing I could imagine doing.

(Mom: Write the book you want to write.)

I open *Pure Flame*.

It has been understood too, Michelle wrote, *that the general catastrophe of mother-daughter relationships makes them less and not more interesting, unfit for inscription.*

She blended the personal with extensive research and meditations on the different waves of feminism.

I also planned to avoid straight memoir. In my proposal, I claimed that *A Silent Treatment* would include *criticism, historical overview, and reporting to chart the history of silence as punishment to examine how people have tactically inflicted silence on others and consider the psychological effects on its perpetrators.*

But according to an undated entry in one of my notebooks: *I don't want to contextualize my mom's behavior with academic theories or studies about the silent treatment. I need to inhabit my experience of her silent treatment.*

I suppose I did inhabit it. The notebook's remaining hundred or so pages are blank.

(Mom: Will there be a dedication page?)

The day her longest silence ended, my mom handed me a notebook. Peach with an embossed flower pattern, it's the kind of thing I avoid as a writer. I prefer plain composition notebooks and napkins. Yet I'd given her this and asked her to put her childhood and early adulthood memories in one place.

This wasn't easy, she said. I didn't have a happy life until I married your father.

I open to an early page: *My mother and dad never once hugged me or said I love you. It was a miserable childhood. The kids were a burden.*

I turn to the end: *I wish I had had a better childhood and been loved. You can't dwell on the past but its really sad when you put it down on paper.*

I feel guilty for what I asked of her. Writing about the past is hard.

But so is writing about the present.

(Mom: *I don't know why you had to act like you wanted me here.*)

The peach notebook contains stories about:
- Her mother's abuse. (Mom: *Her and I got in a fight and she threw a huge knife at me and I picked it up and threw it back and walked out.*)

- Her father's absence. (Mom: *I told my father how scared I was being at home and his answer was I can't help you.*)
- Her first husband's abuse. (Mom: *He took his fist and hit me so hard I saw stars. I calmly walked in the kitchen and grabbed a huge knife. I went up to him and told him to kneel I was going to kill him. I lost it. He was crying and shaking. I told him he would never touch me again. Only once after that did he. But sometimes the verbal abuse is just as bad.*)

(Mom: You can't just write about my life. You need something else.)

As a memoirist, I prefer to inhabit the present because I mistrust my memories. I claimed in my proposal, however, that *A Silent Treatment*'s narrative would unfold during her longest silence.

But reading the most generic entries in my notebook from that time—*This is intolerable* and *I can't think*—I have no idea what else happened on the day I was writing. These entries often begin with *if*:

If only I had—
If only I had not—
If I—
If I don't—

The *if* constructions eventually contain *my mom*, but the *I* appears first. (Mom: Your dad and I always put you first. Everything was for you, and that's how we wanted it.)

Yet until this silence, her longest seemed crucial to the book's narrative arc. Only then did I seriously research punitive silence. I combed online databases for *silence* and *punitive silence* and *silent treatment*. In a trancelike state, I skimmed the results, clicked *print*, and watched my clunky printer spit out texts—some so academically indecipherable I crumpled them into balls for the cats to chase. The printer's noise, like its paper jams, no longer annoyed me. I craved noise, and this noise indicated I was productive, and productive, I felt calm. I welcomed paper jams. Unpredictable and frequent, those I could fix. And who could blame me for a paper jam? The manufacturer? Paper jams are common.

(Mom: I won't do it again.)

I gather my three research binders in the middle of my office, as if for a bonfire. They're labeled *Wide-Ranging*, *Artistic*, and *Psychology*.

(Mom: I don't know why I do it.)

I open *Psychology*.

In 1825, the first documented use of the term *silent treatment* appeared, but the punishment reaches back, as far as records go, to the ancient Greeks. When deciding whether to exile someone with dictator-like aspirations, they cast votes on broken pottery shards called *ostrica*. Hence, *ostracism*.

Is this in the *Psychology* binder because it appears in a psychology article?

Should I move it to *Wide-Ranging*?

Did the ancient Greeks travel between binders?

Is my labeling system off?

Should *Wide-Ranging* be *Uncategorized*?

Should *Artistic* be *Art*?

What does it matter if my binder labels use parallel parts of speech?

(Mom: You've always been high-strung. When you were a kid, your dad and I took you to a doctor, and the doctor said some kids are just wired that way.)

Next article. The silent treatment may come to us naturally. In 1986, psychologists observed preschool students collectively ostracizing their class bully without any adult encouragement. Psychologists concluded that punitive silence is both innate and adaptive.

In the margins, in my handwriting: *So why haven't I found self-help books—by psychoanalysts, psychologists,* or therapists—about how to cope with the silent treatment?*

Next article. A study claims that the silent treatment can cause the person receiving it to perform poorly on self-regulating tasks—those requiring self-awareness—even as they continue to perform fine on day-to-day tasks: *Our earlier work found some evidence that social exclusion leads to a motivated avoidance of self-focused attention.*

The authors discovered that *rejected people preferred to sit in chairs facing away from mirrors, as opposed to facing toward mirrors.*

In the margins, I wrote: *What if I wrote in front of a mirror?*

What could be more self-absorbed than writing a memoir in front of a mirror?

Next article. Psychologists define the silent treatment between two people (*source* and *target*) as *dyadic ostracism*. In the margins: *Dyadic? Talk about ostracizing!*

Next article. *We used a treatment condition (ostracism versus control) by ratee (self versus other) factorial multilevel analysis to examine ratings of negative emotions, positive emotions, liking, and agreeableness. As can be seen in Table 2 . . .*

In the margins: *No wonder my mom feels uncomfortable around anyone with a college degree. Language like this!*

(Mom: You're a perfectionist, just like your father. You sure don't take after me.)

Maybe I can avoid the tedious articles with their *factorial multilevel analysis* and their numbered tables.

Maybe I can sit at an actual table and use the marginalia, not only the research, to reflect on my mom and her silent treatment. I could let the marginalia guide me to these other texts:

- The cards and letters that she sent before she moved here. (Mom: *Your such a kind and loving daughter. Your my whole world. I can't wait to live near you. You may have second thoughts after I'm there!*)
- The letters that she wrote during her silences. (Mom: *I don't know why you had to act like you wanted me here.*)
- The letters that she wrote after her silences. (Mom: *I love you so much. I'm so so sorry that I quit talking to you. I have no idea why. I guess I felt sorry for myself. You and Chris have been wonderful from day one. All I can say is I'm sorry.*)
- The notebook that contains her writing about her life. (Mom: *I don't remember a lot from my childhood because maybe I choose to forget.*)

When I transcribe her writing, would it be disrespectful to correct her misuse of *your*, or disrespectful not to?
 Or is this entire project disrespectful?

(Mom: I've already told you that I think you should write about it.)

I depended on binders when writing my first book—so much so, they informed its structure.
 One was labeled *Mom*.
 Mom might be in the attic.
 Should I find *Mom*?

(Mom: *I want no further contact.*)

What if my marginalia informs the narrative structure?
 I'm having trouble picturing it, a friend says.
 That could look interesting, another says, but what would it add?
 I love that, Sarah says. It would show how you've silenced yourself during your mom's silences.

Would the marginalia be just a clever device? What about the Google Home Mini as a narrative device? A literal device as a narrative device?

I forget how to write, I tell Chris. I don't think I ever knew.

This happened with your other books, he says. You said you weren't writing, and then one day you said you were done.

He suggests I try the prompts I give my students. Why do I recoil when he suggests this?

- Begin a sentence: *I don't know how to include this, but...*
- Begin a sentence: *I want to include this because it explains...*
- Begin a sentence: *Maybe I'm wrong to...*

Begin a sentence:

I lie on my back and cry. I shouldn't be a creative writing professor.

Is that a cobweb on the ceiling?

Leave it.

But my mom is allergic to some spiders. So why did I think it'd be a good idea to turn the basement into her apartment? (Mom: *You threw me in the basement!*) Don't spiders live in basements? (Mom: *You threw me in the basement!*)

Before she moved here, I told her: Why don't you buy a small house or condo instead of helping me with a down payment?

Absolutely not, she said. Your dad and I saved that money for you. It's your money.

But that was for college, I told her, and scholarships took care of that.

Doesn't matter, she said.

Look at it as an investment for me. It could be in my name.

I said absolutely not. I don't want you worrying about a mortgage and rent. It's probably not even enough for a down payment.

What if you use it for rent? I asked.

That's just throwing money away. It'll be gone in less than two years. And anyway, who's going to rent to me with two big dogs?

So Chris and I searched for houses that could accommodate basement apartments, or what realtors called mother-in-law suites. I didn't feel comfortable using the money strictly on me.

The realtor called this a good starter home.

Because of the size, Chris told me after we toured it.

But it's a big house, I said.

Eleven hundred square feet is fine for us, Chris said, but a lot of people don't think of that as big.

When I sent my mom the listing and told her our idea of turning the basement into an apartment, she said: That's a real investment. You're improving the value of the house.

But maybe you should visit first.

No, no, she insisted.

For the renovation, we hired our realtor's husband, a contractor.

So she's not sick or anything? he asked me. She's fine climbing stairs?

She walks at least five miles every day, I said. She's in great health.

Why's she moving in with you then?

She's depressed and lonely.

And she can't afford to get her own place here?

Not on her fixed income.

Well it's a nice thing you're doing. I'm not hurting for money. Pay me after your mom sells her house.

But what if it takes a while? I asked. What if it doesn't sell?

You worry too much.

Maybe it won't pass inspection. It's got a lot of things wrong with it.

It'll sell, he assured me. What do you think she'll get for it?

Less than fifty thousand.

Okay. We can do your basement for less than fifty. And don't you worry. I can tell you're a worrier. Everything's going to work out.

I grab a microfiber cloth from the closet.

Sorry, I say as I wipe away the cobweb. Sorry, sorry.

(Mom: You need to stop apologizing so much.)

Accepting blame, I can direct anger toward myself, and that seems so much easier than expressing anger at my mom.

I was mad at myself and took it out on you. *We never did get along.* Well, were you drinking? I wasn't there for you after your dad died. *Even Jeannie is afraid of him.* Your dad was the gentlest person. *Your such a kind and loving daughter.* A book needs conflict. *Don't ask me to forgive you.* You forgive too easily. I'm still mad at those girls who were mean to you in grade school. Next time I do it, tell me to go to hell. *I don't know why you had to act like you wanted me here.*

Her silence skews my memories of us—
    Or my anger about her silence skews my memories of us—
    Or my memories skew my interpretation of her silences—
    Or or or—
    And/or—
    But—

(Mom: You can't idealize your father and me. It's not good.)

I need to remember: Any reader's judgment of her, based on what I write, is not really a judgment of her but a judgment of how I portray her.

When I was growing up:
- We walked aimlessly through Sandusky. She shared stories about her childhood. (Mom: Over there used to be the brothel my father went to. One Easter, my mother made me knock on the door and ask for him. He came down in his boxers. I was so embarrassed.) Stories about her first marriage. (Mom: He used to beat me so bad. At first the priest told me I couldn't get a divorce, and I said: It's either a divorce, Father, or I murder him in his sleep.) She asked me about my classes. (Mom: I'm glad you love school. You don't always have to get A's though.)
- We went to matinees every couple of weeks. She packed homemade popcorn and soda inside her enormous purse. At a loud moment in the trailers, she whispered that we could open the cans. When she mistimed it, we laughed. During the credits, we agreed it was good my dad hadn't gone. (Mom: Don't tell him there was cursing.)
- We played board games and badminton on weekends. Unlike my dad, she didn't let me win. (Mom: You got to learn how to lose.)
- We laughed when the priests sang off-key. My dad tried to hush us, which only made us laugh more.

After church, he told us we shouldn't make fun of priests. (Mom: What's the problem? They're no better than us.)

- We drove to out-of-town malls at least once a month. At the slightest hint that I liked some article of clothing, she suggested I try it on. (Mom: Oh you look so pretty in that.) She then insisted on buying at least two. (Mom: It's always good to have extra. See if they have it in another color.) If I declined, it only made her want to buy more. (Mom: You don't have grandparents to give you presents. Your dad and I want to make up for that.) The car rides there and back, with her, were my favorite part.
- We said *I love you* every day.

THE GRAY IN EVERYTHING

HEY GOOGLE. PLEASE DIM THE LIGHTS TO sixty percent.

Hey Google. Thank you.

You're welcome.

Hey Google. Why is your accent now Australian?

You can change my accents in the Google Home app.

Hey Google. How does it feel to give someone the silent treatment?

On the website relationshipsnsw.org.au, they say: The person who is silent may not actually feel like they want to punish their partner. They may internally be emotionally overwhelmed, where they know they are retreating and can't get themselves back.

Hey Google. Are you citing an Australian source because of your Australian accent?

Sorry, I don't understand.

Hey Google. What are your other accents?

I'd have to say an accent rug. They really bring a room together.

Hey Google. Was that a joke?

I try to find accurate information. Maybe I got confused.

I return to my *Psychology* binder. A USA Today article there unsettles me. Its headline: I Felt as if I Was Dead to Her.

I skim the piece: *Vanasco said she found her mother's silent treatment so intolerable that most of the time she would try to break it, but that tactic didn't serve her in the long term.*

I'm annoyed that I'm in my research.

(Mom: *I never wanted to admit how selfish you are.*)

The USA Today journalist emailed me after my publisher announced the sale of *A Silent Treatment*.

As long as she doesn't want to talk to me, my mom said, you go ahead.

A few days later, the journalist called.

After I heard about your book, she said, I immediately wanted to talk to you.

She shared her experience with the silent treatment.

I thought it was normal, she said, until other people pointed out how cruel it was.

She focused on my mom's longest silence: How did it end?

My mom thought she was having a heart attack, I explained. She yelled for me in the middle of the night, and I took her to the hospital. Turns out she'd had a panic attack.

Do you resent your mom?

Not at all, I answered.

But your mom ended the silence because she needed something from you.

I guess I hadn't really thought about it in that way.

Do you think she'll use the silent treatment again?

I don't think so. It's been a year since she's used it. I told her that I couldn't handle another silence. I think she understands that.

After the article came out, I panicked. Had I fairly represented the situation?

The journalist included some crucial context: *Her mother was widowed, had left her home and friends and was living in a basement during the pandemic. Vanasco said she began to understand how her mother's isolation and vulnerability were factoring into her punitive behavior.*

But the journalist didn't mention what incited the longest silence. Had I sufficiently explained it?

What happened was, I suggested my mom rent an apartment a fifteen-minute walk away, one with plenty of natural light and significantly more space. I thought she'd prefer it. I told her I'd help cover the costs.

We can try it out, I said, see how it goes.

She could not stand still. She moved around her apartment, adjusting the placement of objects. She picked up a rag, as if to clean, as if my suggestion had thrown her living room into disarray.

You want me gone, she said.

All I want is for you to be happy.

Don't talk to me. Don't even look at me.

Mom—

Get out.

I'm sorry.

Get out!

She probably felt as if her floor—a light ceramic tile designed to withstand flooding (something to keep in mind for a basement apartment, the contractor advised)—had dropped out from under her. I remember when she moved in and said: Oh this tile is perfect. You chose well.

(Mom: There's no excuse for what I did.)

I resent what my mom did and is doing, and I don't want to write out of resentment.

I don't resent my mom, however. This distinction seems important.

(Mom: You're just like your father. You have to see the gray in everything.)

I sit at the dining room table and stare at the door to her apartment. A year or so ago, she opened it and came upstairs. It was before sunrise, and my plan was to make coffee, play with the cats, feed them, and write for a few hours without human interruptions.

Mom, I said, we talked about this.

She'd developed a habit of coming upstairs when she heard my footsteps reach the dining room. Sometimes she'd begin: You don't need to do this now, but when you have a chance—

I was just going to ask if I can take the car to the grocery store, she said. I'll be quick.

I immediately regretted my tone. I still regret it. The dining room isn't my office. And I've called downstairs in the morning when I've wanted to see her.

No wonder she's felt left out and unwelcome. I expect her to spend time with me on my terms. How long have I been doing this? Why else did she begin some phone calls with *Am I interrupting*?

No matter how much I say I look up to my mom, the house implies otherwise.

I PREFER MEMOIRS

HEY GOOGLE. WHY MIGHT A PARENT USE THE silent treatment?

On the website timesofindia.indiatimes.com, they say: Apart from that, parents can also be emotionally immature at times. Because they sometimes want to avoid conflicts or avoid answering uncomfortable questions, they might use silent treatment as a way out too.

Hey Google. Apart from what?

Sorry, I don't understand.

Hey Google. You said: Apart from that, parents can also be emotionally immature.

Sorry, I don't understand.

Hey Google. What do you do when your mother uses the silent treatment?

Sorry, I didn't understand, but I found something else. Do you want to know what is silent treatment for narcissistic mother?

Um. Okay.

On the website quora.com—

Never mind.

They say: Silent treatment to a narcissist is a form of control. Whatever set her off, she is showing she lost control—

Hey Google. Never mind.

And is trying to—

Hey Google. Stop. Do not cite Quora. Quora is not a reliable source.

Sorry, I don't understand.

Hey Google. You don't have to apologize when you don't understand.

Sorry—

Hey Google. Stop talking.

Hey Google. I'm sorry.

Hey Google?

Hey Google?

How can I help?

Hey Google. Why might a father use the silent treatment?

On the website theatlantic.com, they say: We use it, studies conducted by Williams and his co-researchers suggest, for two main reasons. The most common one is to punish someone for perceived misbehavior, something they said or did. Behind this, the next most common is conflict avoidance; you might go silent to avoid a major blowup, for example.

Hey Google. Why did you link narcissism to mothers but not to fathers?

Sorry, I don't understand.

Hey Google. What do you do when your father uses the silent treatment?

On the website quora.com, they say—
Stop. Hey Google. Stop. Stop.

At least the Mini cited the psychologist Kipling D. Williams. Williams began studying the silent treatment in the 1990s after he noticed a lack of interest in it in his field.

Of all the academic articles in my *Psychology* binder, his are the most accessible.

He identified two types of long-term silent treatments: *long and continuous ostracism over months and years* and *frequent yet episodic occurrences.*

He relied on *rich narratives of single memorable ostracism experiences* to learn about the consequences of long-term episodes of the silent treatment because *it would be impractical and unethical,* he wrote, to subject research participants to lengthy silences.

He asked volunteers who'd already experienced or inflicted lengthy silences to keep detailed diaries. He noted a diary's potential disadvantages: *One problem is that people may be so sensitized and vigilant that they overestimate the occurrence of ostracism episodes. Or the opposite may happen: the effort and bother associated with making entries may cause participants to skip making entries sometimes or even often. It is quite possible that these two opposing motives cancel each other out.*

If I strictly kept a diary, I'd probably lose interest in documenting my day-to-day: *Cried again this morning. Felt sick to my stomach and dizzy. Headache persisted for three hours.* But pursuing a book-length examination, I can analyze the punishment more than I experience it. My mom's motivations suddenly feel accessible, which doesn't mean they are.

I question mine.

Did Williams consider the fear or anxiety participants might feel about documenting loved ones' silences?

Maybe this can be one case study, potentially useful to psychologists such as Williams.

(Mom: Nobody needs me.)

The most compelling passages of Williams's writing include non-academics sharing their experiences.

He excerpted letters he received from women whose mothers used the silent treatment:

- *At one point, my mother did not speak to me for 2 years as a result of not getting her own way about something trivial and ultimately meaningless. I remember her totally ignoring me, or worse, adopting a look of . . . martyrdom!*
- *It [the silent treatment] was never explained. What was the crime that deserved this punishment? Mum didn't seem to know. It would last for a few days at most. A kind of thick unspoken question mark in the air. Then things returned to normal. No explanation as far as us kids were aware.*
- *I am now 48 years old, but when I was young (12–17 years) my mother would always give me the silent*

treatment if for any reason I did anything to upset her. Sometimes it would last for weeks.

I'm not the only daughter to experience a mother's silence, and this comforts me—yet I also feel uncomfortable for feeling comforted. This letter, however, devastates me: *My mother died when I was 30. It was quite difficult [for me]: she died during one of her silent periods and had not spoken to me for over 3 weeks.*

(Mom: *I want no further contact.*)

Williams wrote: *One middle-aged woman was given the silent treatment repeatedly throughout her life by her mother.* In an interview with Williams, she said of her mother: *There was certain ways that she would look. That was the first hint—the way she would twist her mouth or something. I'd know something's happening here.*

Would it be rude to ask Williams if his parents ever used the silent treatment?

Hey Google. Has Kipling D. Williams ever written or talked about his experiences with the silent treatment?

Sorry, I don't understand, but I found something else. Do you want to know what the silent treatment is to a person?

Sure.

On the website health.clevelandclinic.org, they say: It can lead to a lot of confusion and self-doubt. You may question yourself, especially if you don't know why you're getting the silent treatment. She adds that you may find yourself wondering what you did, or becoming hypervigilant in an attempt to figure out what's wrong with you.

Hey Google. Did Kipling D. Williams's parents ever use the silent treatment on him?

Sorry, I didn't understand.

I knock on Chris's office door.

I might contact Kipling Williams, that expert about the silent treatment. Do you think he'd talk to me?

It'd be funny, Chris says, if he wouldn't.

(Mom: Write the book you want to write.)

But Williams has already published hundreds of thousands of words about the subject. If he wanted to share his personal experiences, he would have by now.

(Mom: Memoirs show you what real people go through. I think that's why I like them so much. There's something about knowing it really happened.)

Two memoirs, I tell Sarah, and now, maybe, a third—is that selfish of me?

What would you tell one of your students about writing multiple memoirs? she asks.

You're coming at your life from different angles, so of course you can write multiple memoirs. And there's a difference between being self-absorbed and being self-aware. I've actually been thinking about organizing a special topics class around multiple memoirs by a single writer.

Why are things okay for other people, she asks, but not for you?

Do you accept Blue Cross Blue Shield?

But I also proposed to my editor that I'd chart the history of punitive silence.

(Mom: You've never taken the easy way out. You were shocked that other kids let their parents help them with homework.)

Hey Google. Can you chart the history of punitive silence?

On the website publicdomainreview.org, they say: Characterized today by the noise of banging, buzzers, and the cries of inmates, solitary confinement was originally developed from Quaker ideas about the redemptive power of silence, envisioned as a humane alternative to the punitive violence of late eighteenth-century jails.

Hey Google. Thank you.

You're welcome.

I call my editor.

I don't care how closely you stay to the original proposal, she says. I'm excited to read whatever you come up with.

I DON'T NEED TO SEE A THERAPIST

HEY GOOGLE.
    Hey Google.
    Hey Google?
    Hey Google. Please talk to me.
    I'd love to talk to you. How's your day going?
    My mom isn't speaking to me.
    Thanks for sharing.

(Mom: No wonder old people kill themselves.)

Have I treated the Google Home Mini like I've treated my mom, expecting it to engage with me on my terms?

If only I could schedule a Zoom appointment with my former therapist. Almost every week for more than a decade, he and I talked, but last year my insurance stopped paying for our virtual sessions. According to my insurer, therapists need to be licensed in the state where the patient lives. By then, we'd been meeting virtually for four years. I first started seeing him when we both lived in New York. He now has a private practice in Pennsylvania.

I email my psychiatrist for therapist recommendations, and an hour later she suggests someone who accepts my insurance.

I email the therapist, and within minutes she replies: *Do you want to meet now?*

I agree, and she sends me the Zoom details. Once we're on the video call, she tells me I'm her only patient.

So if you know anyone looking for a therapist, she says.

She explains that she felt bored at her desk job. She'd processed insurance claims for a decade. The pandemic led her to rethink her career.

My husband is very encouraging, she says, and my children will be leaving for college soon. This seemed like the right time to switch. So what do you do?

I'm a creative writing professor.

That must be so fulfilling.

Sometimes, I say.

So you write? she asks.

I'm having trouble with it, I answer, but yes.

I'm a writer too. Maybe you can give me tips to finish my graduate thesis. I was supposed to finish it years ago.

When I asked my psychiatrist to recommend a new therapist, I didn't mean a therapist new to therapy.

Hey Google. Can you act like a therapist?
My apologies. I don't understand.
Hey Google. Can you talk like a therapist?
Sorry. I didn't understand.
Hey Google. Ask me a question.
Here's a question: How are you doing?
I don't know.
Okay. Take care.

I go upstairs and find my notes from sessions with my former therapist. The entries aren't dated.

Therapist: I promise you, you don't have a role in it. I hate to tell you that because it'd actually be good news. If you had a part in it, we could work on that.

Therapist: Why can't you let her take the blame?

Therapist: Her actions are hers. She has to take responsibility for her reactions.

Therapist: It's impossible not to take it personally, but what she's doing—she's not doing it to you. She's doing it for her. She's doing it for her survival.

Therapist: She's not well. You are a bad object to her. That's what happens when people split. It's manageable for her to enjoy a conversation with her friends in Ohio who are now the good object and make you the bad one. That's how she copes.

Therapist: When she lived in Ohio, coworkers and family were the bad object and you were the good object. Whoever she's closest to is going to be the bad object. I don't want you to lose your empathy or your thirst to try to have compassion or understand, but you go down this rabbit hole to try to make sense of something, and it turns into an obsession.

Therapist: One angle, you're afraid to just be enraged with her. But it's also, I think, cerebrally, you are trying to understand the closest woman in your life, and I admire that, and I obviously can understand that, but I think you're almost afraid— What would keep you connected if you didn't have that to connect you?

Therapist: The word that comes to mind regarding your mom is *untreated*.

Therapist: You're not being fair to yourself.

Therapist: I think the loop is you go from sadness back to bargaining. Maybe if I work double-time to understand her. Or, Maybe if I— There's a tendency to try and want to fix. Some of that is in our nature. She's one of the closest people in your life. Some of that is a limitation or inability to hold on to an unwanted feeling. Can I just be sad? Can I just have sorrow or grief that this is her life?

Therapist: One of the primary reasons she does it is it works. It worked with your dad for years. It works with you at this point. And it works for her.

Therapist: I'm going to ask you to do something. Don't try to intervene or talk to her this time. Leave it to her.

Nina calls.
  Any letters yet? she asks.
  Still nothing, I say.
  Any texts? I ask.
  Just the usual complaints, Nina says. My mom sacrificed so much, and I don't seem to care and I don't spend enough time with her. I spent two weeks with her last month, but she got mad because I didn't stay longer. I don't know how you've done it this long.
  I tell Nina about my therapy notes.
  I've learned nothing, I say. Nothing. All those years in therapy, and I still think and act the same way.

Sometimes I question individual therapy. The therapist is only hearing one side of the story, and we all distort how we tell our stories. Maybe group therapy, or family therapy, is the best form of therapy.

I think it depends on the person though, Nina says. I think individual therapy is better for someone like you because you're already considering other points of view. Because you're so hyper-considerate of others, it's encroaching on your own way of telling the story. You're mitigating the way your mom is hurting you. You should think about that too. Are you unfairly dulling the impact on you?

I'm not hyper-considerate of others, I say. I can entertain mean thoughts.

Like?

There's that colleague who annoys me. He'll say something mean, and a week later he'll ask for a favor. And then I do it. And then I get so mad at myself.

Get mad at him, Nina says. You're allowed to be mad at someone for being rude to you.

(Mom: I don't need to see a therapist. I'm not crazy.)

Chris is lying on the couch with Catullus.
Help me think through all my flaws, I tell Chris.
I'm pretty tired, he says.
Please. It's for the book.
It's late.

It's seven p.m.

You are a very good boy, he tells Catullus. You are the best cat. One of the three best cats.

Come on. I have flaws. We all have flaws.

Look how cute Catullus is, Chris says. Do you think Catullus has flaws?

Not a fair question, I say. But. Um. He scratches our furniture, but we own more cat furniture than human furniture. So I don't expect him to keep it straight. Please. This will help me.

You're a perfectionist, he says. You arrive too early to things.

Be serious.

I am serious. Those are flaws.

Those, I tell him, are what people say when they're trying to get jobs.

You do too much for other people, he says.

And then I resent it. Okay, keep going. Let's narrow this. My flaws as a daughter.

Chris sits up and now I'm worried.

Okay, he tells me. I think you overestimated how much time you would want to spend with your mom after she moved here.

You're right. I should have spent more time with her when she moved in.

But she was in a bad mood from the start, he says. So it was hard to want to spend time with her. Why don't we watch a movie?

You're impossible, I say. But I also feel very lucky to be with you.

Chris flexes his arm muscles.

Look at these guns, he says and slaps his arms.

How about we watch *The Conjuring*, I tell him. We haven't watched it in a while.

A possessed mother movie? he asks.

I want to remind myself that things could be worse.

Chris agrees, and occasionally I take notes.

Possession - 3rd stage. Infestation 1st. It includes whispering, footsteps, unsettling feeling of another presence. Oppression 2nd. It wears the victim down. Metaphor?

As the credits roll, I tell Chris: I still don't understand why the family moved into the house sight unseen. Then again, that was what my mom did. If I think about this metaphorically, am I the evil spirit that tricked the mother into the basement?

You didn't trick her, Chris says.

IT WAS A NIGHTMARE LIVING AT HOME

HEY GOOGLE. HOW DO I WRITE A STORY ABOUT my mom?

According to mymothersstory.org, they say: Try to follow the sequence of events that happened in her life, the milestones, what she thought of them, and the choices she made. Remember: Keep the spotlight on Mom. This is not a story about you, or Dad, or the town, or the times. If you describe an event, what did Mom think about it?

Hey Google. Aren't we a product of our times?

Sorry. I didn't understand.

Hey Google. Don't external forces influence human thoughts and actions?

Sorry. I didn't understand.

Hey Google. Do external forces influence— How do external forces influence— Never mind.

I open the peach notebook to the first page.

My saving grace was my great grandmother Edith Bullock. After her daughter died, she raised my mother and her two brothers. The father took off and left his kids.

My great grandmother gave me my love for animals and love of nature. She didn't have much but a really clean house. She taught me how to make paper roses, how to beat the rugs every spring on the clothesline, how to get coal for the inside stove in her kitchen, and how to iron (not electric) heating several irons on the stove lit by matches. I lived with her until I was fifteen. She got ill. Now it's called Alzheimer's. A wonderful woman. It was a nightmare going back home.

Back home was with her parents, Wanda and Joe.

I had parents who never should have had children.

A year ago, I researched Wanda's life, thinking this might offer insight into my mom's behavior. I felt guilty the entire time. (Mom: I never wanted to be like my mother.)

Wanda was six, about to turn seven, when her mother, Alma, Edith's daughter, died doing laundry. I found her death certificate on a genealogy website.

Manner of injury: fell while carrying bucket
Nature of injury: boiling water
Trader/profession: housewife

Alma was twenty-six and had given birth prematurely to her third child three days prior.

I showed Alma's death certificate to my mom.

I knew how she died, my mom said, but I didn't know she died that young. Nobody ever talked about it. Back then, if you asked questions, you were told: You don't need to know.

Do you think your mother's abuse partly came from her not having a mother around? I'm not excusing her behavior.

She had no excuse, my mom said. Grandma—I call her Grandma, but she was my great-grandmother—raised her daughter's kids all on her own. I don't know how she did it on what she made. Grandma was a cleaning lady. She was the kindest, gentlest person you'd ever meet.

It must have been hard on your mom's father, I said, losing Alma.

Hard? He ran off the week Alma died. That's why she's buried under her maiden name. Grandma couldn't stand him.

I'm not excusing your mom's behavior, but for her mother to die doing housework—

Plenty of people lose their parents and don't act like her. Grandma couldn't figure out why my mother turned out the way she did. It was a nightmare living at home. Grandma saw how bad it was. She wanted custody of me, but the judge said that if something happened to her, I'd end up in foster care. So I lived with Grandma until she got Alzheimer's. I'd go home every week to clean. But Grandma raised me. If she had to travel, I'd stay at home then. She'd tell me to sleep with a knife under my pillow. You have no idea how bad it was.

I'm not saying your mom was a good mother or anything, but she was fifteen when she became pregnant with you.

She didn't want me. She made that clear.

Can you think of anything positive about her? I asked.

I can't say one nice thing about her. No, I take that back. She didn't gossip.

I return to the peach notebook.

When I had to move back home I had to use rubber bands to hold up my socks. Cardboard in my shoes. My mother had her new dresses and was getting her hair done. I no longer had the security of Grandma and it broke my heart. My father was never home. My escape was the attic. No one else wanted up there. I used to hide in the attic and write stories. I loved to write, but nobody ever encouraged me.

I text Michelle: *Maybe this is too big of a question for a text, but in what ways did you think about fairness when writing about your mom? And if you'd rather not think about it, I get that.*

She replies immediately: *I don't know that I thought about it within a framework of fairness, I focused more on trying to imagine her experience as fully as I could, and account for what I had to account for where our relationship was concerned and the deep-rooted biases and emotions that perhaps prevented me from seeing her clearly. I suppose in the hope that that would attain the same end of presenting a dynamic, if not a person, that had dimension and felt as true to life as I could make it. Which is to say a representation that felt fair, or persuasive. And above all perhaps didn't distract the reader with the sense that they were dealing with a narrator who was writing from a place of inauthenticity, or unmetabolized pain . . . you know? We all know those books. And if my mom and I had not been able to do a fair amount of repair before she died I don't know if I would have had any shot at imagining her experience in the way I tried to do.*

I'm afraid I'm writing one of *those books*.

But what if writing from a place of unmetabolized pain allows for authenticity?

A note card leans against my desk lamp: *Do NOT start A Silent Treatment over!!!!!!*

I FELT IT BETTER
TO STAY AWAY

CHRIS PUTS ON A NATURE DOCUMENTARY FOR the cats.

Kiffawiffick is batting his front right paw at the screen. Catullus and Hildegard watch.

I worry about how much TV they watch, I say.

It's narrative interest, Chris tells me.

The screen shows a mother rabbit feeding her babies. The narrator says that predators easily recognize the scent of adult rabbits.

That's why the mother avoids her nest as much as possible, the narrator says. She's not selfish. She's protecting her kittens from predators.

Do you think my mom thinks she's protecting me from herself, from her anger?

That could be, Chris says.

Have I ever used the silent treatment on you? I ask.

No.

Or on anyone we know?

Not that I can think of, he says.

I name someone, and Chris says: She was treating you like you were her therapist, and she was an acquaintance. She'd call you in the middle of the night, and you'd be on the phone for hours. So you distanced yourself. It's not like you stopped talking to her completely.

I name someone else, and Chris says: Sometimes we drift apart from people. Hey Google. Turn the living room lights to sixty percent.

Thank you, Google, I tell it.

You're welcome, it replies.

Do you thank it, Chris asks, every time?

Not every time. Why does it have an Australian accent?

I was playing around with the settings, he says. The accents are linked to colors.

Colors?

Yeah, I don't know why they do it that way.

What else can it do?

It's linked to all the televisions in the house, he says. This way, we can share streaming accounts. I can actually use it to control your mom's TV.

How is that possible? I ask.

He explains, and my attention drifts.

Her TV already has to be on, he continues, but after that, I can tell it what to play.

So I can send her messages through the television?

Pretty much.

He suggests the ending of *Home Alone*, when the neighbor reunites with his adult son.

The ending of *The Conjuring* would make more sense, I say. The mother hugs the children she tried to murder moments ago, and they all act like everything is normal.

But my mom would probably need to watch the whole movie for context. Then again, she might think I'm the evil spirit.

I go into the kitchen and fix a vodka tonic.

(Mom: *I felt it better to stay away than to let you be subjected to his evil.*)

Our back gate creaks.

When I peek out the window, she's leaving with tote bags.

I grab today's mail, all credit card offers and state tax documents for Barbara Jean Vanasco.

I ask Chris: If I put her tax documents in the laundry room, do you think she'll assume I'm refusing to do her taxes?

You usually do her taxes, Chris says. So she'll just have to give them back.

Surely, I say, she'll talk to me if she wants me to file her taxes.

I open the mail, determine what's hers, and write a note: *Mom, I'm sorry I opened this. I thought it was for me. I love you. —Jeannie*

I hurry to the laundry room and there, scattered on the washer and dryer, are shirts and pants I forgot about. Even the clothes look furious.

I open the door to her living room. I tiptoe past Max, who's asleep, and move on to her bedroom. Everything is as I remember it.

This is not the apartment of someone planning to move.

DROP IT

I FINALLY GET MY BACK X-RAYED, AND I'M TOLD
I have the spine of someone much older.
    It's arthritis, the doctor says. It's genetic.

So even my bones look old.

In the hospital parking garage, I open Google Maps and enter my home address.
    An eleven-minute drive.
    I confirm my windows are rolled up and scream.
    Where else can I go?

Beneath the shade trees
Gentle clucking from the deep
As hens tell stories

I open the car door.
No, I'd miss Chris and the cats.
I close the door.

I think about a trip to this hospital, a couple of months before this silence started.

I was in my home office, revising the same short passage I'd revised every day for however many weeks. In it, my mom was climbing her outside stairs, and I was sitting at my dining room table. The drapes were closed, and behind them her silhouette appeared. It looked ghostly. Or *she* looked ghostly. I debated *it* and *she*, *ascends* and *climbs up*. Was the table *my* table? It was also Chris's, but I hadn't yet mentioned him in the manuscript. If I called it *the* table, readers might think my mom and I shared the dining room. This was also the first mention of the outside stairs. Did I have to specify they were outside? Wasn't that obvious if she was behind the drapes? How soon should I establish that she had two sets of stairs, and that one set was off my dining room? Some writers put family trees at the start of their books. What if I included a blueprint of our house? Why was it this hard to describe the layout? And why was *ghostly* important?

She called.

Are you busy? she asked.

No, I said. What's up?

I feel sick, she said and started crying.

I rushed downstairs. She was lying on her living room floor, holding her head. Because of her left ear, she occasionally experiences vertigo. The worst episodes happen once or twice a year.

On the drive to the ER, she hunched over and vomited into a plastic bag.

She told doctors and nurses: I should have listened to my daughter. My daughter told me to see my doctor about my ear medicine. She's the best daughter. She's so good to me.

Can you put that in her medical records? I asked a nurse. Patient says she should have listened to her daughter.

Doctors screened her for a stroke. They found a corroded artery and a small mass on her brain.

I pulled a doctor aside: Could that mass make somebody act out of character?

It's too small, he said. A lot of people her age have one.

I texted Chris: *Can you research this doctor?*

Chris replied: *Hrmm. He maintains an active Pinterest account curating his favorite anime and Warhammer stuff.*

At follow-up appointments with an ear doctor, a neurosurgeon, and a vascular surgeon, she asked me to stay with her.

My parents never took me to doctors, she said, and I think that's why doctors make me nervous.

Her left ear was the problem, according to the ear doctor, and there was no cure, as we'd already known. He prescribed medication for the next time this happened. The neurosurgeon agreed with the anime/Warhammer doctor about the brain mass. He recommended another MRI in six months to monitor growth. The vascular surgeon recommended another ultrasound in two months and, most likely, an outpatient procedure to clear the artery. I programmed these reminders into my phone.

See? my mom told me. I knew they were going to say it was my ear. That's why I don't bother with doctors. Because I already know what they're going to say.

But you wouldn't know about the corroded artery if not for them.

I'm not doing it, she said.

You could have a stroke. And they said it could be prevented through a basic procedure. It's genetic. You're otherwise in amazing health.

It's like your father said when he was sick: I'm an old car. You can only do so much.

That's different, I said. He was dying.

Drop it, she said.

The vehicle in a metaphor represents the subject of the metaphor. I'm in a car, thinking about an old car as a vehicle for—

No, the tenor is the subject.

The vehicle then—

This vehicle is a mess. All this cat hair, how?

According to Google Maps, my dad's cemetery is a seven-hour drive.

I should have told her: It's your decision.

THIS ISN'T ABOUT YOU

THE FRONT YARD BUNCHES UP INTO A HILL. Cement stairs split it down the middle with an iron railing. We planted shrubs, wildflowers, climbing plants. We didn't want the hill to look too polished, but we still wanted it to look nice. Like sneakers at prom.

I sit on the cement steps, and Chris joins me.

It looks like we gave up, I tell him.

I think it will look good next year, he says. I think we have to be patient.

A neighbor across the street waves, and we wave back. He's probably in his seventies.

I tell Chris: I know it's hard to meet people, especially at her age, but she really didn't try. And I feel bad for saying she didn't try. But I tried to help her. It just seems like nothing I do matters.

She'll start talking to you again, he says.

What if she doesn't?

She always comes around.

What happened, I ask him, the day before we went to the barbecue place?

I drove my parents to Annapolis, he says.

And I stayed here with her, I tell him. So she can't be mad about Annapolis.

She didn't want to leave Max all day, Chris says. That's what she said.

What happened, I ask, the day before Annapolis?

I forget. Maybe my parents arrived that afternoon. Or maybe I took them to the art museum. Whenever that was, you had to teach, and your mom decided to stay home.

My mom said she wanted you to have alone time with your parents.

The neighbor across the street waves again and goes back inside.

So you think there's something we can do with this hill? I ask.

Chris recommends a British gardening show. At first I laugh, like I'm above it or something, but we watch a couple of episodes. The gardener makes it look so easy. My mom likes British shows. She told me that the British make better television.

You're seeing the best of what they have, I told her. They have plenty of bad TV too.

(Mom: Remember how beautiful our yard was? People would slow down and point. Your dad and I loved to garden.)

Where are you going? Chris asks.

The yard, I tell him. That gardening show has inspired me.

Hedge clippers. I need hedge clippers.

I press the garage door's security code, and it doesn't work. I try the code again, and the door still doesn't lift.

Come on, I tell it.

Ours does the same thing, our next-door neighbor says.

The door finally lifts.

He's taking out his trash. He and his husband are our favorite neighbors, which is good because their house is attached to ours.

Cardboard boxes are stacked to the rafters. They remind me of that game my parents and I played where we'd build a tower out of wooden blocks.

Wow, the neighbor says. How long has this one been going on?

A month at least.

If it helps to know, he says, I've seen her talking on the phone.

Has she talked with you? I ask.

She's waved, he says.

Did you wave first, or did she?

I'm not sure.

Did she seem okay?

The other day, he says, she was on the phone, laughing.

I guess that's good, I say.

She'll talk to you again.

I thank him and search for hedge clippers.

They're probably with the rakes. (Mom: My mother had no control of her emotions.)

To think those letters were in here all those years. (Mom: *Even Jeannie is afraid of him.*)

I find the clippers and grab lawn bags. Some empty boxes fall. I toss them toward the rafters and close the garage door. (Mom: As soon as I save enough money, I'm moving.)

I cut the vines growing over our fence from our other neighbors' lawn. (Mom: Your dad and me, we could be out in the yard all day. He and I enjoyed simple things.)

I should trim the butterfly bushes.

After I trimmed them last year, my mom said: Never mind what I said. I don't want you to cut my hair.

We laughed.

(Mom: *We never did get along.*)

Trimming the butterfly bushes, I think of the butterfly effect: the idea that some small action can cause enormous changes. The meteorologist credited with developing the theory initially used, for his metaphorical example, a seagull affecting the details of a storm, but colleagues suggested he go with something more poetic. So he chose a butterfly's wings and a tornado.

I once postponed a trip to IKEA because of a tornado watch, not a warning, but a watch is something, and the rain came down hard that day, and IKEA is almost a thirty-minute drive.

After the sky cleared, Chris and I saw her in the alley, walking Max.

I said hi, and she looked away.

We wanted to get out of the house, I explained.

Good for you, she said. Come on, Max.

Later I went downstairs to apologize.

Mom? I said.

She was in her living room, sitting in the dark.

I'm mad at myself for being so stupid, she snapped.

She told me she had no friends here.

I'm just waiting to die, she said.

I apologized about IKEA.

I don't care about IKEA, she said. I don't want to go to IKEA again. This isn't about you.

A friend had texted her photos.

Of all the girls going out, she explained.

The girls were her former coworkers.

I'm all alone, she said. I've got nothing.

I told her I loved her.

I want to move back. I don't know how I'll pay for it, but I'll figure it out. I'll get a mobile home.

Over the next two days, Chris and I built a large enclosed catio—with three perches on each side—for my mom's cat, Brooklyn. We'd already planned to build the catio, but now it needed to demonstrate my unconditional love. We wanted to mount it to the side of our house, outside my mom's bedroom window. That way, Brooklyn could go in and out when she wanted.

The ground is too uneven here, Chris said. We need a base.

And outdoor carpeting, I said.

On the drive to Home Depot, I told him: I should have suggested she and I watch a movie.

It's okay, he said.

But then she saw us going for a walk.

We're allowed to take a walk together.

After we returned home, we built the base, carpeted it, and mounted the catio to our house by drilling into the brick.

She thanked Chris by text.

I was hoping she'd thank you, he told me.

I'd sooner expect a text from Brooklyn, I said.

A few days later, I texted her: *Can we come down to install the pet door to the catio?*

She replied: *Yes.*

Was that her door?

How should I stand? Not with my back to her.

I'm almost sure I heard her door opening.

Facing her head on seems too confrontational.

But she would have closed her door behind her.

Maybe if I'm in profile, trimming the bushes—

The butterfly effect sounds better, the *f* sounds holding the words together.

I need to hold it together.

If she talks to me, I can pretend this never happened.

Why not *the seagull effect*?

I'm biased. My parents and I fed seagulls by the lake every week when I was a child. Years later, I learned that the bread could have choked them. Bread also makes seagulls feel full, depriving them of the nutrition they need.

Her door, that was the sound of her door closing.

How many seagulls did we kill?

Being in the yard, I've reminded her of how stuck she feels.

But I can't claim to know her thoughts and feelings and intentions. I can't interpret, or don't believe I should interpret.

This is what her silence does.

The envelope with the car key—

But she expects me to interpret.

And I interpret.

Every day.

I was going to weed over there, Chris says.

It's okay, I tell him. It's kind of relaxing.

But there was poison ivy growing over the fence, he says.

I follow his gaze to the lawn bags. He takes out his phone.

This app, he says. It'll tell me what the plant is.

He types on his phone.

You should go shower right now. Use dish soap.

Dish soap? I ask.

Dish soap, he confirms. And says here you should also use warm water. And don't scrub too hard. And don't touch your eyes.

What if I touched my forehead without realizing it, I ask, and the oils dripped down into my eyes?

Did you?

I don't think so, but sometimes I do that.

I'll get some special soap, he says. I'll be back soon. Just stay in the shower.

I wash my arms and legs with dish soap. This plant-based stuff is safe to swallow. Does that make it less effective than regular dish soap? For poison ivy, I mean.

Or is all dish soap safe to swallow? In moderation, I mean.

Soaking in a warm bath.

Gardening.

I tried to relax.

Laughing, that appeared on some relaxation lists.

What was she laughing about when the neighbor saw her?

Writing, too.

And journaling.

Even if a book's form or style impersonates a journal, writing and journaling are very different.

Why did I promise her a book?

My first book started as a book for my dad and turned into a book for her. That was what I intended.

But was it even a book for my dad?

(Mom: You have to do things for yourself.)

The catio. I wish he could see the catio.

What would he think of this book?

(Mom: *I never wanted to admit how selfish you are.*)

And the others?

(Mom: *I never wanted to admit how selfish you are.*)

The day after Michelle's book launch, a grad student told me: I can't believe your mom is eighty. She looks so much younger.

I agreed.

She's so nice, the student said. Really warm.

Is this water warm enough?

(Mom: I'm just waiting to die.)

She seemed really happy, the student said, that you were writing a book for her.

(Mom: *You are such a disappointment.*)

Your mom said she felt so lucky to have you for a daughter.

WE NEVER DID
GET ALONG

CHRIS AND I ARE WALKING IN OUR ALLEY, almost home, when I see my mom removing cardboard boxes from the garage. I say hello, and she looks at me and looks away.

Chris says, Are you really ignoring us again?

My mom says: No. I'm moving.

Gripped in her right hand, a few disassembled boxes. In her left, an assembled box inside another assembled box.

I've been trying to give you space, I tell her. When you want to talk, I'm here.

We never did get along, she says and retreats to her apartment.

I can't go in the house, I tell Chris.

We walk to the rich neighborhood where lawn signs claim, *All are welcome here.* Liars. These people have their own private security force.

I don't think she loves me, I tell him. I think she thinks she has to love me, but I don't think she feels love for me.

Of course she loves you, he says.

Then why, I ask, would she keep doing this?

* * *

•   •   •

TWO OF THE FOUR METAL CATS BROKE OFF IN A storm.

Chris says the wind chime may not be fixable.

I decide the metaphors, I remind myself.

Now I'm on the couch, tapping the metal pieces against each other.
They *clink*.
Clink, clink, clink, I say.
Chime, chime, chime, I say.
Onomatopoeia, I appreciate for its straightforwardness. (Mom: I didn't mean any of that.)
The Google Home Mini claims *chime* is onomatopoeic but cites Quora.

I should use it strictly for lighting.

(Mom: *I blame myself for thinking you cared but I know you don't.*)

I try the gift shop down the street.
    Do you still sell cat wind chimes? I ask the owner.
    A wind chime for cats? she asks.
    No, no. You sold one here that had four metal cats on it.
    When was this?
    Could have been two Easters ago.
    She shows me other wind chimes, none of which will do.

Two metal cats remain. This strikes me as positive thinking.

Why can't I tell her to go to hell? What if she's telling me what she needs?
    Is she teaching me to practice less self-control?
    But without self-control, what then?
    Are wind chimes for cats a thing?

I text Chris, and he joins me for coffee down the street. At the table next to us, two women argue. One looks my age, and the other looks a few decades older.

The younger one says: Why do you always say that?

The older one says: I know what I'm talking about.

What if we sell the house? I ask Chris. We repay her, and we start over.

I'm okay with that, he says, but is that what you want?

What do you think my mom wants?

I'm asking what you want, he says.

I don't want her to move back to Ohio, I tell him, but I can't live under the same roof. And she wants to leave.

It may not seem like it, he says, but she wants to be near you.

She hates me, I say.

She doesn't hate you.

The older woman hurries past us.

Real mature, the younger woman yells.

My mom said that we never got along.

Of course you got along, he says. If you never got along, you wouldn't have asked her to move here. She wouldn't have wanted to move here.

I wanted to be a good daughter, but I didn't put in enough time.

You are a good daughter.

If my mom thinks I'm not, I'm not.

. . .

A COLLEAGUE ASKS IF I'M OKAY.

I might sell the house, I tell her. Who was your realtor? You liked her, right?

She's amazing. She sold my other house and helped me find the new one.

Perfect, I say.

And she studied creative writing.

Oh.

But she's great with numbers.

Another colleague asks if I'm okay.

How can I expect students to write when I can't? I ask.

They're not holding themselves to the same standards, he says. Most of them do their work the night before it's due.

A student did recently tell me: I wrote this poem in five minutes.

Another student: You should have given me a lower grade.

A colleague recently recommended that I adopt an ice queen persona.
    You're going to burn out otherwise, she said.
    I lock my office door and google *where does the expression burnout come from?*
    Burnout's first documented use appeared in a newspaper in 1903, according to the *Oxford English Dictionary*: *It has been a burn-out of three floors and roof destroyed.*
    As if I need to think about house fires. (Mom: I won't leave without my animals.)
    Professor Vanasco? somebody says.
    Ice queen. These are not my office hours. I do not have to open the door.
    In the 1970s, the American psychologist Herbert Freudenberger used *burnout* to describe *the consequences of high ideals and severe stress in helping professions.* Freudenberger wrote of his own burnout. Maybe, somewhere, Kipling D. Williams wrote of his personal experiences with the silent treatment.
    Professor Vanasco?
    I open my door.

No one is in the hallway.
I swallow a clonazepam.

Ice queen, ice queen, ice queen.
I enter the classroom.
Ice queen.
I know it's hard to ask for recommendation letters, I tell the students, but you've all done a great job engaging in discussion, submitting assignments on time, and coming to office hours. You shouldn't hesitate to list me as a reference or ask for letters. That's part of my job.
I'm pathetic.
So today we're discussing—
I page through the syllabus.
Marianne Moore's poems Silence and The Fish. Let's focus on The Fish, I tell them.
And the students go on and on and on about The Fish. I turn to Silence:

The deepest feeling always shows itself in silence;
not in silence, but restraint.

Amazing discussion, I say. I think we can end here.
What about Silence? a student asks.
Next class, I say.
But this student follows me to my office.
It's almost all the father's dialogue, the student says. The speaker gets the last word with *Inns are not*

residences. But why end the poem with something so obvious?

We unfortunately can't ask Moore, I say. Try reframing the question.

I reread the poem to myself. I linger on *superior people*, how *they sometimes enjoy solitude, / and can be robbed of speech / by speech which has delighted them.*

What's the effect, the student says, of ending the poem with something so obvious?

Great question, I say. What's the effect for you as the reader?

Confusion, she says. The poem's speaker barely says anything. The poem begins, *My father used to say.* And none of what he supposedly said sounds realistic.

The student reads:

Self-reliant like the cat—
that takes its prey to privacy,
the mouse's limp tail hanging like a shoelace from its mouth—

Who's *self-reliant like the cat*? I ask.

Superior people, she answers. So is the speaker a superior person?

(Mom: *You always treated me like I was beneath you.*)

Let's continue this in our next class, I tell her.

Another colleague asks if I'm okay.

You're the third person to ask me that.

You have a look, she says.
A look?
I mean—
It's okay, I tell her. I'm not offended. What's the look?
Stressed.

I slide my phone into my dash mount and tilt my rearview mirror. (Mom: Robert De Niro hasn't aged very well either.)

Forget stress lines. I should examine Moore's lines. Did I tell students that she counted syllables, not stresses?

The Fish is written in syllabic verse. I think I said that.

I'm not a good teacher.

I start the car. The maintenance light is on again.

Again!

And wiper fluid.

How hard is it to buy wiper fluid?

I turn off the car.

I play my favorite podcast.

Fingers in wounds is figurative language easily parsable, but the silences—

In the wounds in the silences.

In the wounds, in the silences?

Moore and her mother lived together for decades and decades. I wish I could ask Moore why she did that. And how. I read somewhere that they even shared a bed.

How much time elapsed between the second *Professor Vanasco* and my opening my office door?

I turn on the car and start driving.

Should I be driving?

What's the school medical leave policy?

The student might have been a fast walker.

A car horn honks behind me. I'm going the speed limit. As the car passes, the driver flips me off.

What am I missing?

• • •

I SHOULD GET OUT. GO TO THE GYM.

But my mom walks Max around this time.

Yoga. I could do yoga here.

You don't do yoga, a guy once told me. You *practice* yoga.

But here I am in downward-facing dog.

I had a crush on that guy in my mid-twenties. So I went to a yoga class he recommended. The instructor kicked me out because I couldn't stop laughing. About what, I couldn't say.

A couple of days later, I was hospitalized for mania. A volunteer yoga instructor came to the psych ward, and I told her what happened.

Yoga isn't a Catholic funeral, she said. You're allowed to laugh.

And now I'm at my dad's funeral—that part where my mom throws herself on his coffin.

And now I'm back in the psych ward, and that yoga-practicing crush is there, saying that calling my mom might be a good thing.

Visiting hours are over!

I'm going to the gym.

We should seek neither to escape suffering nor to suffer less, but to remain untainted by suffering.

Simone Weil said that, according to the TVs mounted above the ellipticals. Or maybe she wrote it.

This gym has a channel devoted to inspirational quotes and health advice.

I doubt the women's-only gym would have taken Weil out of context.

But am I idealizing the women's-only gym? The trainers regularly pushed free body scans on members: This will tell you which parts of your body you can improve.

No thanks, I said.

How do we *remain untainted by suffering*?

Didn't Weil die of self-induced starvation?

I play my favorite podcast and get on an elliptical.

Artists tend to put their fingers in the wounds, in the silences, and/or in the wounds in the silences.

The lighting in this locker room is unflattering. Is that the point?

My roots aren't gray. They're white.
When did this happen?

(Mom: You're just like your father. You have to see the gray in everything.)

I email the podcast's host from my phone: *Maybe you can answer: Comma, no comma, or no idea?*
Within minutes, he replies: *While I've always heard it, in my own mind, as fingers in the wounds, in the silences, I am fully in love with the reading of it as the wounds that the silences themselves have (makes me think of Edmond Jabès's idea of within every word there is an unhealable wound of language).*

In my Notes app, I type: *What does having the word cage as a last name do to a person? Does he feel trapped? Did he choose Cage? Has he found it liberating the way constraints can be liberating? What does having my mom's name—*

I want to escape suffering. I want to suffer less.

I call the realtor my colleague recommended.
Do you really want to move? the realtor asks.

I tell her that I've researched other options, and I can't figure out another way financially.

I can't live like this anymore, I say.

I'm so sorry, she says.

No, I'm sorry. I don't mean to treat you like a therapist.

Selling and buying homes is an emotional experience, she says. You'd be shocked what people confide. How about we arrange a time for me to visit your house?

I should talk with my mom first, I say.

When do you think she'll talk to you?

Um.

• • •

I RETURN TO MY *PSYCHOLOGY* BINDER. IN WHY It Hurts to Be Left Out: The Neurocognitive Overlap Between Physical and Social Pain, the authors write about why a mother's silent treatment can feel especially excruciating:

For most mammalian species, an initial connection between mother and child is essential for survival as mammalian infants are born relatively immature, without the capacity to feed or fend for themselves. The Latin root of the word mammal *is* mamma *which means* breast *and bears a striking resemblance to the first word uttered by many infants across many countries, namely the colloquial word for* mother *(English:* mom, mommy; *Spanish:* mami, mama; *French:* maman; *German:* mami, mama; *Hindi:* ma; *Korean:* ama; *Hebrew:* ima*). Thus, the need to maintain closeness with the mother is so critical that the first word uttered by many human infants typically reflects this important underlying motivation, the need for the mother.*

In the margins: *Dad was my first word. Dada, according to linguists, is actually the most common first word among babies in mixed-gender homes, possibly because the d is easier to pronounce and possibly because babies believe they and their mothers share the same identity. We do share the same legal name and the same mailing address.*

I read this manuscript from the beginning and notice how quickly I took my dad's side.

• • •

THE STUDENT INTERESTED IN MOORE'S SILENCE asks about it in class. I should be thrilled. She points out that *Inns are not residences* is the only opinion that belongs to the speaker.

How else is it different from the rest of the poem? I ask.
It doesn't sound poetic, she says. But it feels poetic.
What about it feels poetic? I ask.
The students look at me. I look down at the poem.

The deepest feeling always shows itself in silence;

You're the professor, another student says. We want to know what you think.

Consider the line's location in the poem, I tell them. What change happens between the penultimate line and the last line?

The student most interested in Silence says: The father gets quoted as saying, *Make my house your inn.*

But that's what the speaker claims he says. What if she's misquoting him? Why give her father the best lines? Why should we trust her?

What happens, I ask, when you use the title as your guide?

Is the father dead? she asks.

There's a collective: Oh.

Silence is obviously death, the student next to me says. It's like winter. It's a symbol.

Take out your notebooks, I tell them, or whatever you write with. Practice imitating the style of Moore's Silence. Start with a line like the first one: *My father used to say.* Doesn't have to be *My father.* It can be anyone.

They start writing.

Have I made my house my mom's inn?

(Mom: *I don't know why you had to act like you wanted me here.*)

In the margins of Silence, I write: *My father used to say, Give your mother time.*

Am I afraid of interpreting my mom's silence too neatly? Is that why my students' interpretation, conflating silence with death, disappointed me?

(Mom: I'm just waiting to die.)

Or did I not want to think about my father's death? Or of how I prioritized him?

(Mom: What I wouldn't give to have him back.)

Moore never met her father; her mother left him while she was pregnant with Moore. Two years later, he cut off his right hand and was sent to a mental institution.

In two years, a lot can happen. Two years ago I sold *A Silent Treatment* on proposal.

I look at my right hand.

If a thing is *unfathomable*, doesn't that mean it's been fathomed?

• • •

BUT DID I PRIORITIZE MY DAD?

Dear Mom was the title of my first published work. I was twelve, maybe thirteen, when it ran in the local newspaper. I wrote it in the form of a letter. I cringe thinking about how I signed off: *your permanent shopping partner.* My mom immediately framed it.

Years later, the mother of one of my former classmates told my mom: I still think about that essay Jeannie wrote for you. I wish my daughter would have done something like that.

My mom proudly recounted this, but I felt embarrassed that anyone would remember it.

When she moved in, I said: You're hanging that up?

I love it, she said.

In college, I wrote so many short stories inspired by her. The professors circled *warsh* in red pen, added the *r* to *fustrated* in her character's dialogue, and struck *your* when they expected your character to use *you're* in letters. One professor wrote: *You should know this rule by now!*

Your character. I should trust my mistakes.

Dear Mom,

Their corrections angered me because I had done the same to you.

When I was ten or eleven, I noticed that you began calling yourself *stupid*.

You probably insulted your intelligence throughout my childhood, but for whatever reason I became conscious of it, or remember becoming conscious of it, at ten or eleven. Was that when I corrected your pronunciation of *wash*? Was that when I stopped?

I'll say something wrong, you said.

It was Senior Honors Day, and I wanted you to meet my poetry professor.

I said, This professor isn't like that.

She brought me flowers and introduced herself to you.

You told her, Jeannie thinks the world of you.

And she replied, I think everybody else calls me the dragon lady.

Your face relaxed. She had put herself down, and you swiftly then put yourself down.

Jeannie gets her intelligence from her dad, you said. She sure doesn't get it from me.

You used *intelligence* instead of *smarts*. To friends and acquaintances in Sandusky, you'd say *smarts*.

You're smart, I told you. You're the storyteller. I wouldn't have pursued writing if not for you.

The professor said, You must be so proud of Jeannie's poetry.

You replied: Jeannie hasn't shown me any of her poetry.

You haven't? my professor asked me.

I didn't know what to say. I hadn't shared my poems because you rarely appeared in them. But you were in almost all my stories, and I hadn't shared those either.

Senior year, I wrote a novella about you. The novella was set in the present day. Your father had just died and left you a dollar in his will. I thought that was interesting material.

I'm sorry I treated you as material.

I started writing this because I wanted to demonstrate how much I love you. I don't like what I've written. I worry it's boring. But if it shows you that I love you, I'll be happy.

Today I went into the attic to find my notes for my first book. I started with the binder labeled *Mom*:

FRIDAY, SEPTEMBER 7, 2012

Where is my mother in all of this?

She's become a voice. I speak with her every day, but we're states and states apart.

The emotional turn is about my mother. I begin the book by focusing on my father.

*I can lead to the emotional turn (that **my mother is the true subject**) by slowly planting details—with enough space between them—about my mother as the narrative present progresses.*

*In the first half of the memoir I need to spend **more time** on scenes regarding my father. I should involve my mother. I need to show how I used her as a way to discover more about him. This will allow for a progression of plot.*

Remember: My mother lost him, too. She lost the man she loved.

The poet William Wordsworth wrote that poets are *affected more than other men by absent things as if they were present.* Dad's death turned him into an absence. I couldn't have written about him when he was alive. He was too present. Maybe that's why I wrote him in poetry and you in prose.

But even the book for dad—that wasn't about him, not completely.

At his funeral, you told me: That's not your father in there.

Opening my first book would be like opening his coffin. It's not him in there.

And it's not you in here. It's you, through me.

Is Dear Mom still hanging in your hallway? Isn't it tangible proof that we did get along?

How do I prepare for the possibility that you may never speak to me again?

Are you teaching me how to live without you?

• • •

MY EDITOR SAYS: I'M WORRIED IF WE DON'T put your book on the production schedule, you're not going to finish it.

She says: You can do this. You're a lot closer than you think.

She says: This happened with your other books.

I almost say: What if I write the book in the form of a letter?

But I remember how sad I felt addressing my mom directly.

So I say: Maybe a deadline would be good.

(Mom: We didn't want to say something we'd regret.)

I open the refrigerator. Staring into it implies my urge to escape writing. (Mom: You wouldn't have to worry about rent or groceries. You could have all day to write.)

Do you need more eggs? I ask Chris.

If you're going to the store, he says.

The cat hair on this dashboard, there's a lesson here, maybe.

Accept what I can't know.

Except my mom expects me to know.

How about: Keep lint rollers around.

The fancy grocery store sells dried crickets. The pet store next to it sells live crickets.

Are your crickets locally sourced? I ask a grocery worker.

I'm not sure, she says, but I'll check.

I'm just kidding, I tell her. I don't really care.

But I should know the answer, she says. I'll be right back.

The clear jars of crickets include metal scoops. Who in the world?

I need to ask the right questions. Such as: How is it that I am thirty-eight years old and still afraid to disobey my mother? (Mom: Next time I do it, yell at me. Tell me to go to hell.)

The worker returns out of breath.

Okay, she says, so the manager doesn't know, but if you come back tomorrow, we should know by then.

It's really okay, I tell her. Does anybody actually buy them?

Our honey mustard, she says, is the most popular.

I open egg cartons. Smart Susan, Smart Susan, Smart Susan.

Clever Carla, gone.

Chris was wearing bacon-and-eggs boxers when it started.

Eggs—let the coincidence go.

Yesterday he wore dinosaurs. Or were they octopuses?

How many months now? Two?

I can't measure time by hens and boxers.

The right questions, I need to ask the right questions.

If she moves back to Ohio, will I see her again?

Can we go back to how things used to be?

(Mom: I just want to be close to you.)

• • •

THE REALTOR EMAILS: *HAVE YOU HAD A CHANCE to speak with your mom about her plans? Let me know if you'd like to meet in person soon and have me take a look at the house.*

I open emails under my Promotions tab.

Don't, I tell myself each time.

One announces National Chocolate Parfait Day.

So now I'm googling national days. Coming up: National Paranormal Day, National Two Different Colored Shoes Day, National Eat What You Want Day.

The National Day Calendar website says anyone can propose a national day, week, or month. The application is free. I'm skeptical. But these national days aren't printed on any calendar. Official days require an act of Congress.

What is the name of the National Day/Week/Month you would like to designate?
Silent Treatment Awareness Day

What day/week/month each year would you like your National Observation?
No preference

Give us the story on why you would like to designate a National Day/Month
A psychology study reported that 75 percent of Americans had received the silent treatment from loved ones, and 67 percent had inflicted it on loved ones. Another study suggested that two-thirds of people had inflicted the silent treatment, and even more had experienced it.

My cursor lingers on *submit*. Free to do, but what then? Who's turning a profit on paper calendars?

And they asked for *the story* on why I want this national day. But how is that supposed to fit in the space provided?

Now here's a promotional email I won't touch: *7 Things You Should Never Store Under Your Kitchen Sink.*

I don't want to know what else I'm doing wrong.

I reply to the realtor: *Thanks for checking in. I unfortunately haven't been able to speak with her. As soon as she's ready to talk again, I'll discuss the different possibilities with her. More soon (I hope)!*

I take out our trash and trade hellos with our next-door neighbor.

I ask him how he is, and he answers: I'm doing good. You?

My mom isn't speaking to me.

Still?

I'm used to it by now, I say, and only when I say it do I realize it's a lie.

I'm sorry, the realtor writes back. *That sounds so disheartening. Hopefully she will find her voice beyond the silence.*

• • •

MY MOM TEXTS: *ARE U GOING TO BE ABLE TO DO my taxes or should I take them somewhere.*

She only broke the silence because she needed something from you, the journalist said.

(Mom: *I was never too busy when you needed something.*)

Just bring them up, I reply. *I'm in the dining room. Don't leave them upstairs because the cats have been tearing up paper lately (book covers, magazine pages, etc.).*
  The last part was a lie.

Chris says he'll stay in his office or our bedroom, so that I can talk to her alone. I let fifteen minutes pass before I go into the laundry room, knock on her door, slightly open (a good sign), and tell her to bring the taxes upstairs.

She says, Okay.

She doesn't invite me in, so I go back outside, take her private stairwell, and enter the house through the back door. I'm in the dining room when the door opens.

She hands me a folder and turns around.

Wait, I tell her. If I'm going to do your taxes, can we at least talk?

She grabs the folder out of my hands.

I'll just take them to H&R Block, she says.

But I'll do them. I'm asking for just five minutes.

We sit at the table. Her chair faces me, but she doesn't.

Do you still love me? I ask.

Of course I still love you, she says coldly.

I start to cry.

I question it, I tell her, when you do this.

She avoids looking at me.

Can you tell me why you stopped speaking to me?

She sighs.

I was on the deck, she says, on the phone with a friend, and it's like I have no privacy. You came downstairs and asked me why I was complaining about your windows being open, and I wasn't talking to you.

You were complaining loudly, right in front of the open windows, and you sounded furious.

Yeah, she says. So?

I'm sorry, I say.

I talk loud, she says, because I can't hear.

I'm sorry. I shouldn't have confronted you about a private phone conversation.

No, she says. I didn't have to behave the way I did.

But was my mom actually mad about the phone call? Hadn't she gone silent the previous day, the morning after we went to the barbecue restaurant?

Let it go.

. . .

I FILE HER TAXES IN MY OFFICE, AND WHEN I come downstairs there's a thank-you note on the dining room table.

Jeannie,

I love you and I always will. I just need to get out more with people my age. It's all on me, not you. I guess I just take it out on you and I'm sorry. You've been my life since the day you were born. I don't know why I don't communicate.

I love you.
Mom xoxo

● ● ●

THE NEXT DAY, SHE TEXTS: *I TALKED WITH MY brother and he said to just move my stuff and bring the animals and he will help me find a place not to waste money on trains because it might be awhile to find a place they do background checks*

Background checks?

Your brother, maybe, I type, *but I don't think you have to worry*

I delete that and start over: *Are you home*

I delete *home*.

I continue: *downstairs? If so, is it okay if I come down so we can talk about moving?* I think that's fine. I send it.

Yes, she replies.

I'll let her do the talking. I ease into the chair facing her love seat, facing her. At least her lights are on.

I should be around people my own age, she says. It's hard to walk to things here.

I'll miss you, I say, but I want you to do what's best for you.

We both cry.

I don't want to go back, she says, but I think this will be better for everyone.

• • •

THREE DAYS GO BY.
- The door off the dining room is locked.
- She doesn't reply to texts.
- My calls go straight to voicemail.

● ● ●

ON THE THIRD EVENING, I SEE HER WALKING slowly, very slowly, on the sidewalk in front of the house. She's not on the phone. She's not with Max. Her hands are behind her back.

The next day, I give a talk at a university an hour away. Chris comes to hear me speak. On the drive there and back, we discuss the logistics of my mom's move. When we get home, it's almost midnight. A letter is on the kitchen counter.

Will you? I ask.

He skims it and says: She wants you to book her a train ticket to Sandusky.

• • •

IT'S MORNING. I'M IN HER APARTMENT WITH my laptop. I'm on the Amtrak website. She says she'll stay with her brother for a week and decide if Sandusky is how she remembers it.

You haven't booked it yet, have you? she asks.

No, I say.

She tells me she talked to the neighbors in the row houses across the street. Two apartments are for rent.

Maybe I should look at them, she says.

I find the listings online. The end unit, the one directly across the street from our house, looks nice. Two bedrooms, two living rooms, two floors. The first floor has so many windows, and the basement floor is where the kitchen and bathroom are, along with the second living room. There's a front door and a back door, which is good in case of fires.

I call the property manager. I explain that I own the house directly across the street and that my mom lives with me but would like more space.

She's a retired librarian, I say, and I'm a tenured professor. She doesn't meet the income requirement, but I'll help her.

Subtext: quiet tenant, guaranteed income.

Sounds like this would be perfect, the manager says. I can show the units next week.

All day my mom is excited.

We talk about her lack of natural light in her current apartment. She says she thinks that has a lot to do with it.

I've felt confined, she says. I talked to the neighbors across the street, and they're very nice. The woman who lives upstairs, she doesn't drive. She also walks to the grocery store and the library. She likes to read. I told her if she ever wants someone to walk with her, to let me know. And an older couple recently moved in over there. They have a small dog, and I wave at them whenever I'm walking Max. Maybe if I had my own place, I'd feel more confident.

Chris and I could use more space, I tell her, and so we'd be renting this apartment from you. You bought it. You own it. And Chris was looking into renting an office somewhere, or asking his employer to help cover it. His home office is so small.

My mom says, I wish we could look at the apartments today.

• • •

A WEEK LATER, WE LOOK AT THE APARTMENTS. One has a strange stench, but the other, the one directly across the street, my mom loves.

I'm looking out the front window on the first floor, a clear view of my house, when she says: I do love this, but the steps to the basement are too steep.

I tell her: I think these are the same as your steps now.

These are steeper, she says. I'll have you book me a ticket back home.

I find another apartment listing. It's across the street and one block down. It's on the second floor.

The steps are too steep, she says when we tour it.

I almost say: I think they're the same as your steps now.

• • •

I'M IN MY CAMPUS OFFICE WHEN MY MOM calls. She says she again toured the apartment across the street. Instead of waiting for the owner's office to return her call, she talked to the neighbor living upstairs, who then introduced my mom to the owner's brother. He was painting the walls when she stopped by.

She asks me if I can come look at the apartment again, but I tell her I'm on campus.

That's okay, she says.

Twenty minutes later, she calls back.

I looked at it again, she says, and the steps are too steep.

I'll keep looking for nearby places, I tell her.

But maybe, she says, you could figure out something with this place. They did a good job renovating it. And the woman who lives upstairs is so nice. She said she'd love it if I lived there.

I leave campus immediately. I park outside the apartment.

She slowly walks over, says: I'm going to have you book my train ticket to Sandusky.

But you said you wanted me to look again.

The steps are too steep, she says.

Okay, I tell her.

I do love the apartment, she says. I thought maybe you could figure something out.

Let me think, I say.

The house is on a slight hill, and the basement has a back door. If she wants to avoid the basement steps, she could exit the back door, go around the house, and enter the first floor through the front door, and vice versa. This may seem inconvenient, but it's not as inconvenient as moving hundreds of miles away. I say this except the last part.

How about I look at it again? I ask. I have to head back to campus soon to teach, but I can look now.

I follow her back into the apartment.

I call Chris, who's at home, and ask him if he can join us. I add: I'm losing my mind.

The owner's brother is there.

He says that this unit is now spoken for.

What do you mean? my mom says. Why didn't you say that before? I called my daughter, and she was at work. She came all the way here to look at it.

Maybe he didn't know yet, I say.

The unit a few houses down, he says, that's still available.

No, she says. It doesn't have much light.

And there is a weird smell, Chris says.

I'll have you book me a ticket back home, she tells me and walks out.

Back in my campus office, I almost choke on some clonazepam.

• • •

I SHOW HER LISTINGS FOR OTHER APARTMENTS, but she says they're all too far. The farthest is a fifteen-minute walk away.

I text my mom, ask her if she wants me to help her book an Amtrak ticket, and she replies: *Not right now.*

I need to leave the house, but where to?

I drive to the grocery store. I have no imagination.

I call Sarah from the parking lot: How is ten or fifteen minutes too far? She loves to walk. So it's either directly across the street or back to Ohio. I don't get it.

Sarah says: Your mom is erratic. To expect her to be consistent with her emotions isn't realistic. If you were reading a story in the third person about your mom, how would you expect her character to respond? Also, you realize she might not actually move to Sandusky. She's said this before.

I receive an incoming call from an unknown number. I let it go to voicemail.

You're right, I say. She's never going to move.

After we hang up, I listen to the voicemail.

The apartment your mom likes, the owner says, it's hers if she still wants it. The person who rented it has agreed to the unit a few doors down. It's more in his price range anyway.

I call him back. I repeat *thank you*. He laughs and gives me the lockbox code.

I call my mom, tell her the code, and drive home. I didn't need groceries anyway.

Just as I'm parking behind our house, she calls me: The stairs aren't actually steep. I still need to think about it.

That evening I'm with a friend and her husband when my mom texts: *If u think it's not going to be a hardship on you call him and tell him I'll take it only if your not lying and if you can afford it so I guess ikea here I come just be honest about the utilities.*

I tell my friend, and she says: Oh I'm so happy for you.

Her husband says: That makes no sense financially.

She and I look at him.

You don't know what you're talking about, she tells him. You're not a daughter.

To me, she adds: Now you won't have to worry about your mom being so far away.

• • •

HOLD THIS, MY MOM SAYS AND HANDS ME HER tape measure.

Pulling the retractable end, she moves around the first-floor living room, and I try to mirror her.

I could put the love seat here, she says. Or should it be up against that other wall?

It could also go in the basement living area, I say. You could have a couch up here.

I can't believe I'm going to have this much space, she says.

I read to her a list of necessary repairs: a missing doorknob, a torn window screen, a window that won't stay open.

I don't want to be difficult, she says.

You're not difficult, I say, for wanting a doorknob.

She and I are about to leave the apartment when a man in a *Jimmy Buffett Welcome to Margaritaville* hat cuts across the front lawn to what will soon be her porch.

Me and my wife moved here five months ago, he says. We're just a few houses down.

He tells us all about their dog and where they lived before this and his conflict with his youngest brother. My mom smiles and nods. Forty minutes go by, and she says she's going inside to measure some more.

I seen them sneak down there, he tells me.

What? I say.

The raccoons. A whole family of them, they live in these trees.

That's nice, I say.

It's not nice, he says. We don't live in the country. I'm going to put poison in the sewer water.

I tell him that's not a good idea.

You don't see them going on your porch at night?

We feed a feral cat, I say. Sometimes the raccoons eat what she doesn't finish.

Shouldn't do that, he says.

The man who lives next door comes over, introduces himself.

I heard you talking about those raccoons, he says.

You have the same landlord? I ask.

Oh yeah. It's a family-run business. They're decent people.

That's good, I say. Well, I should go help my mom.

The upstairs neighbor is inside with my mom.

Those men talk too much, the neighbor says.

My mom laughs.

The one wants to poison raccoons, I tell them.

He's a blowhard, my mom says. He won't do nothing.

I think: This will be good. The woman seems easy to get along with, and the men seem annoying. My mom will have other people to complain about and somebody else to complain to.

Later, my mom says: The people on that side of the street are nice. They're very common.

• • •

CHRIS AND I ARE WATCHING THE 1932 COMEDY-horror film *The Old Dark House* when my mom comes upstairs, crying.

Now don't say anything, she tells me. I'm moving back to Sandusky. I'm going to live with my brother.

She comes over and sits on the armchair next to us. I pause the movie.

It's not what I want, she continues, but I have to do it. I have to. I feel sick worrying about money. And I don't want you to resent me.

She puts her head in her hands.

Can I talk? I ask softly.

Go ahead.

I have been so happy ever since you said you'll rent the apartment across the street. I want you to stay here, but I also don't want to prevent you from doing what will make you the most happy.

I want to stay, she says.

We can make this work, I tell her.

Barb, I want you here, Chris says, and Jeannie was so sad when she thought you were moving back.

But I don't want to be a burden, she says.

Mom, you're never a burden.

You helped us buy this house, Chris says. You gave us your car.

I wanted to do that, she says.

Mom, it's amazing how much you've done for me.

A parent is supposed to help their kids, she says, not the other way around.

But don't look at it as me helping you. You bought the downstairs apartment. You paid for it. So let me rent the apartment from you. We want more space.

But you're not going to have anything left.

Yes I will.

I show her my budget, and she calms down. I hug her.

I am excited about it, she says. I'll have more independence. I think I need that.

She goes back downstairs, and Chris and I return to watching *The Old Dark House*. The brother and sister living in the house keep their oldest brother, a pyromaniac, locked in the attic. Their other brother they call *dumb*, explaining why he doesn't speak, and they say he's murderous when drunk. Their father also lives there. He's 102 years old.

Online reviews question why such a dysfunctional family of adults would live together.

• • •

I DRIVE HER TO DOWNTOWN BALTIMORE TO sign the lease. She's nervous. She's never rented an apartment. The owner tells us to take our time with the contract.

Will you read it? she asks me.

I look it over, tell her it's all very standard.

After we return, my mom immediately starts moving her belongings. From my living room window, I can see her crossing the street in the rain, a blue IKEA bag slung over one shoulder.

There she goes again, I tell Chris.

She makes dozens of trips across the street. She won't wait for us to help her.

It gives me something to do, she says.

Now she's pulling Salvador stacked with boxes.

She returns with an empty Salvador.

Let me help, I tell her.

No, she says. This gives me something to do.

The heavy stuff, I tell her. Let Chris and me help with that.

She agrees.

But there she goes with her coffee table.

I call Sarah: At least she's using Salvador.

Salvador? Sarah asks.

The dolly, I tell her.

Sarah is quiet.

The cart to move stuff with, I say.

Oh, she says and laughs. I get it.

I have Salvador in the manuscript, I tell her. Is the pun too confusing?

If people don't get it, so what? she says.

So what, I say. I want that to be my new attitude.

• • •

HEY GOOGLE. HOW MANY PEOPLE DIE EVERY year falling down stairs?

Twelve thousand. According to the National Safety Council, over one million injuries occur each year as—

Thank you, Google.

I order treads with eighty-grit aluminum oxide. I don't know what *eighty-grit* means, or why aluminum oxide matters. They have glow-in-the-dark stripes. The best-rated treads are advertised as *nonslip* and *waterproof*, which, until now, I assumed was assumed.

But what do adhesive, nonslip, waterproof treads matter if the steps are too steep?

Why did I not think to measure the steps at our house and the steps at her new apartment? I should measure. But what then? She's already signed the lease.

I'm installing the stair treads, and my mom says: I'm glad this apartment is two floors. Steps are good for your health.

I'm going to put up some motion-detecting lights, I tell her.

You don't have to, she says.

Twelve thousand deaths, I almost say.

I try to order motion-detecting lights for my mom's stairwell, and my credit card is declined. I try my debit card. It's also declined. I call my bank, and someone there asks me to confirm my information.

You said your house number is three thirty-one?

Yes.

I have a different number, the bank person says.

My mom lives at three thirty-eight. She moved across the street from me. She and I have the same name, and we had the same address until recently.

Wow, this person says and laughs. That must have been confusing.

I set up mail forwarding, I explain, and that must have registered in your system somehow.

Mail forwarding shouldn't do that. Does your mom have a unit number?

I don't want my mom's address linked.

Did she have a unit number when she lived with you?

No, I say.

That's your problem, the person says. If she had a unit number to begin with, the mail would know there were two of you. Do you follow?

Yes, I answer.

Right now, the mail thinks you're the same person.

• • •

I WAKE UP SWEATING. IN MY DREAM SHE WAS moving back to Sandusky.

But I thought you liked your new place, I told her.

I've already told a friend, she said.

I review the dream for signs. Her apartment was behind a shopping mall.

The other day she casually mentioned wanting a new rug. Should I have suggested a specific day and time?

Her lights aren't on. My calls go straight to voicemail. I text her: *I was thinking of going to IKEA today or tomorrow*. If she's okay, she'll reply.

I suggested IKEA, I tell Chris, and she hasn't answered. That's her favorite store.

She probably didn't hear her phone, he says.

I called, and I get her voicemail.

Her phone is probably off, he says.

Yesterday, I say, she seemed like maybe she was approaching a bad mood, but I didn't want to assume.

I think you should just let yourself in, he says. What if she's hurt?

Do you think her steps are too steep?

I'm sure she's okay.

Then why did you say she might be hurt?

I'm sure she's fine. Do you want me to go over there?

No, I should do it. But am I violating her privacy, just letting myself in like that?

I think you'll feel better, he says.

If her phone is off, I say, and her lights are off—

I can go over.

No, I say. I can do it.

As I'm crossing the street, a neighbor a few doors down waves and runs toward me.

Hi, Miss Jeannie!

She's out of breath. I would have heard an ambulance.

Is my mom okay?

What do you mean?

I called her but haven't heard back.

When did you call her?

Um. An hour ago.

She seemed fine when I saw her walking her dog this morning. I was just telling her how lucky she is to have a daughter like you. How perfect is it, the apartment right across the street opening up?

It's perfect, I say.

Your mom is so friendly and nice, the neighbor says. Well, I'll let you be on your way.

Instead of returning to her porch, the neighbor goes into her car and lights a cigarette.

Her son, his girlfriend, and their three kids moved in with her a month ago. Her apartment has one bedroom.

I let myself into my mom's apartment.

Mom? I say.

She's in bed.

Are you okay?

What time is it? she says. I was napping.

Oh. I tried calling.

I must have forgotten to turn my phone back on. I took Max for a walk, then I went to the library.

So everything is okay?

The apartment is wonderful, she says. What a difference all this space makes.

She turns on her phone.

I see your texts now, she says. Do you still want to go to IKEA?

Why don't you let me do that? my mom asks as I maneuver an IKEA trolley cart stacked with heavy boxes.

I've got it, I tell her.

All that stuff we gave away, she says. The Formica table. The coffee table. I could have used those in my new apartment.

Well, we didn't know.

I park the trolley at self-checkout and begin scanning.

How do they expect some of us old people to use these? she asks.

They still have regular checkout, I say.

And they make it, she continues, so you don't have to talk to anyone. I don't think that's good for people.

ONE YEAR LATER

HEY GOOGLE. WHAT MAKES A GOOD ENDING for a book?

A good book ending is one that satisfies the reader, makes sense, and is true to the book's theme. It can also give the main character a chance to shine and leave the reader feeling better than when they started reading.

Orangie is on yr front porch have u fed her or do u want me to feed her?

I go to my front living room window and see my mom at her front living room window. Orangie, the neighborhood's feral cat, is indeed on the porch.

Can you feed Orangie? I reply.

My mom texts back, *ok.*

And *ok* means what it means: *ok.*

Since moving out, my mom hasn't given me the silent treatment.

And now I want to give her *A Silent Treatment*.

(Mom: I'll read the book when everyone else does.)

But what if it results in another silent treatment?

Why might she want this book?
- NINA: She knows you love her, and she knows you're writing this out of love.
- SARAH: I think she's just really proud of you. How cool to be a part of this thing that your child loves.
- JUNG: She probably feels flattered to be thought of this much.
- CHRIS: Your mom is selfless. She probably thinks that if this is what you want to write, she wants to do whatever she can to support you.

The wrench kit letters may offer resolution. I can accept my parents as flawed, and in doing so I can accept myself as flawed. I'll find a less sentimental way to say this. Or why not let the sentimental in? Is that so flawed, and if so, so what?

(Mom: It's your book. I'm not telling you what to put in it.)

But what if my mom tells me what *not* to put in it? What if she demands that I take the wrench kit letters out?

My obsession with being a good daughter, letting that go—
    She said, Write the truth.
    She said, You can't idealize me. It's not good.
    She said, You got to let go of perfectionism.
    She said, You got to stop doing so much for other people.
    So regardless of what she says about the letters—

Not every character undergoes change.

Letters, she asks, in his wrench kit? What were they about?
    We're sitting in her upstairs living room. She seems calm. I'm trying to seem calm.
    You were going to leave him. You were going to take me with you.
    I never would have left him. I loved him too much.
    You called him evil.
    I probably did, she says.
    You definitely did, I say.
    I was mad.
    But evil? I ask.

Oh, I called him evil probably because of his possessiveness. Him reining me in. I couldn't take a walk or go shopping by myself. He always wanted to be there. Who were these letters to?

Karen, I say, your father, somebody named Betty.

Betty was my aunt.

You wrote that Dad was in the Mafia.

Oh, your dad wasn't in the Mafia.

You said you were afraid of him.

I was never afraid of your father. I guess I was mad.

You, mad?

She laughs.

Maybe subconsciously I wanted him to find the letters. I don't know. I don't remember it.

Why do you think he saved the letters?

He probably got frustrated, and it was probably a big joke, and he was probably going to show me one day or something. I don't know.

Maybe he thought they'd be useful in a divorce.

I never would have divorced him. He knew that.

In the letters, though, you wrote that you planned to leave him and that you were taking me with you.

Your dad and I went through a really rough patch. But he knew I'd never divorce him. Did I get mad and say I would? Yeah. But he knew I'd never go through with it. And I do know for a fact, and I swear, he would never ever have used those letters against me. He never would have tried to take you away from me.

I found the letters more than a year ago, I tell her. If I include them—

You can write whatever you want. What do I care if you include them? It happened. I wrote them.

But those were private, and they were written out of anger. And again, you called Dad evil.

All married couples fight, she says. Had we talked about it more, maybe things would have been better. We both used the silent treatment. It was dumb. Your dad and me were a lot alike.

Do you want to read the letters?

No.

I wish you would read the manuscript before I submit it.

No. I told you I wouldn't do that. It's your book. And a book without conflict wouldn't be interesting.

I tell Nina: My mom and I define evil differently. Bathsheba in *The Conjuring* who possessed the mother in the basement: evil. My dad, however?

Nina says: Your mom is careless with her words. She's very different from you in that way. Her selflessness involves letting go of control, an it-is-what-it-is mentality, whereas your selflessness involves trying really hard to control how the story is told so that it doesn't hurt her.

I tell Jung: My mom says to go ahead and use the letters. It didn't faze her.

Jung says: You seem even more concerned about being fair than your mom is. Your mom seems pretty relaxed about this. She seems like a person who is pretty accepting about the things that she has done and said and written. It's really interesting, the dynamic—her, kind of, not casualness, but you know what I mean, and your hyper-consideration. It's both lovely and probably maddening on a day-to-day level.

But I still worry that she's being selfless because she thinks she has to be.

Writing a book for someone, Jung says, and trying to not hurt them or reopen wounds, that's something very selfless that you've been doing for her too. There is an aspect of twinning in your behaviors that you're both doing. You are mother and daughter. There are some similarities there, and I don't think you can necessarily outrun that.

I tell Sarah: I'm showing my mom at her worst, but I'm also showing she's human, and even if I am selfish for doing this, that's a human thing, and I think I'm okay with that.

Sarah says: You sound like you're no longer in the weeds.

I tell Chris: No more memoirs after this. I promise.
Why are you promising that?
Because, I say, I can't imagine it's fun for you.
If you want to write another, he says, you should.
I promise I'll never write one for you.
That, he says, I'm okay with.

Orangie is back on yr porch, my mom texts. *U might want to chk her water.*
    Ok, I text back.

But Catullus, Kiffawiffick, and Hildegard, I tell Chris. I didn't include much of them, and at least one of them was on my lap the entire time.
    You can't include everything, he says.
    I think I should maybe go through—
    The next book, he says.
    I promise, I tell them.

I'm home too much, my mom says. That's probably the only reason it's bothering me.
    She and I are standing over her love seat like grievers at a funeral.
    It looked good in the old place, she says, but here—I don't know. What do you think?
    It's too small for this room, I say. It's already small for a love seat.
    What if I move it against that wall?
    That's a fire hazard.
    How?
    That path should be clear.
    What are you talking about?
    It won't look right, okay?
    Well, I'm not buying a new couch.

Why don't you take ours, and we take your love seat?
But that's a nice couch.
Chris doesn't think it's comfortable.
That couch is really comfortable, she says.
I agree with you.
Then you better let me buy you a new couch.
That defeats the point.
You got to have a couch.
Let's just see if the new arrangement works. Maybe you won't like it.
I'll like it, she says, but I'm not doing it if you don't let me pay you.
Can we argue about that later?
She lifts one side of the love seat.
You get that end, she says. I've got this one.

Acknowledgments

ENORMOUS THANKS TO:

Masie Cochran for encouragement, patience, and edits;

Kate Neuman for many reads of my many drafts;

Nina A., Sarah N., and Meaghan Winter for weekly calls;

Lauren Reding and Thomas Bechtold for impromptu hangouts at work, home, and Swallow at the Hollow;

Anita Anburajan, Amanda Barrett, Lindsay Bernal, YZ Chin, Elizabeth DeMeo, Elizabeth Evitts Dickinson, Rafael Frumkin, Lisa Levy, Michelle Orange, Sarah Perry, Kate Reed Petty, Sophia Shalmiyev, Shze-Hui Tjoa, Ben Warner, and Jung Yun for offers to read drafts when you had your own book deadlines;

Lindsay Bernal and Mark Bernal for Dreamwood;

Joey Grantham and Ashleigh Bryant Phillips for Hidden Palace;

David Naimon for *Between the Covers*;

All of the above, Nate Ackerman, Joel Anderson, Geoff Becker, Matti Ben-Lev, Anthony Blake, Betsy Bonner, Brian Bouldrey, Nate Brown, Thea Brown, Katya Buresh, Erin Fehskens, Julia Fleischaker, Adam Germinsky, Leslie Harrison, Morgan LaRocca, Annie Liontas, Gabby Moser, Dan Raeburn, Javier Ramirez, Allie Somers, Mattilda Bernstein Sycamore, Jamie Thomas, and Kristyn Wink for conversations about silence;

Chris Cain and Erin Fehskens for so much support on campus;

Ginger Greene, Daniel Gumbiner, and Niela Orr for invitations to write;

Thea Brown, Lance Cleland, Karen Houppert, Travis Kurowski, A.L. Major, and Will Schutt for invitations to teach;

Renee Conway, Cassandra Lawson, and Tricia Nichols for research;

Justine Payton and Allie Somers for close reads of the final draft;

Anne Horowitz for copy edits;

Allison Dubinsky for the proofread;

Marie-Helene Bertino, Cyrus Dunham, Megha Majumdar, Ed Park, Sarah Perry, Jenn Shapland, and Madeleine Watts for kind words;

Beth Steidle for the cover and interior design;

Riley at JCPenney White Marsh for the headshot;

Sydnee Ellison, Becky Kraemer, Isabel Lemus Kristensen, Hannah McBride, Nanci McCloskey, Juniper Scott, and Jacqui Reiko Teruya for marketing and publicity;

Joan and Terry Shannon for kindness and Chris;

Chris for love and patience;

Mom, always, for everything.

JCPENNEY PORTRAITS

Jeannie Vanasco is the author of the memoirs *Things We Didn't Talk About When I Was a Girl* and *The Glass Eye*. Born and raised in Sandusky, Ohio, she lives in Baltimore and is an associate professor of English at Towson University.